FEEDING THE WORLD

FEEDING THE WORLD

How Innovations in Agriculture Are
Saving the Planet

JOHN F. MONGILLO

BLOOMSBURY ACADEMIC
NEW YORK • LONDON • OXFORD • NEW DELHI • SYDNEY

BLOOMSBURY ACADEMIC
Bloomsbury Publishing Inc, 1359 Broadway, New York, NY 10018, USA
Bloomsbury Publishing Plc, 50 Bedford Square, London, WC1B 3DP, UK
Bloomsbury Publishing Ireland, 29 Earlsfort Terrace, Dublin 2, D02 AY28, Ireland

BLOOMSBURY, BLOOMSBURY ACADEMIC and the Diana logo are
trademarks of Bloomsbury Publishing Plc

First published in the United States of America 2026

Copyright © Bloomsbury Publishing, 2026

Cover design: Diana Nuhn
Cover images:
Top left image © iStock/Kanur Ismail
Top middle image © iStock/onurdongel
Top right image © iStock/PhanuwatNandee
Middle left image © iStock/James Andrews
Middle right image © iStock/PhonlamaiPhoto
Bottom right image © iStock/Scharfsinn86
Bottom left image © iStock/Hiraman

All rights reserved. No part of this publication may be: i) reproduced or transmitted in any form, electronic or mechanical, including photocopying, recording or by means of any information storage or retrieval system without prior permission in writing from the publishers; or ii) used or reproduced in any way for the training, development or operation of artificial intelligence (AI) technologies, including generative AI technologies. The rights holders expressly reserve this publication from the text and data mining exception as per Article 4(3) of the Digital Single Market Directive (EU) 2019/790.

Bloomsbury Publishing Inc does not have any control over, or responsibility for, any third-party websites referred to or in this book. All internet addresses given in this book were correct at the time of going to press. The author and publisher regret any inconvenience caused if addresses have changed or sites have ceased to exist, but can accept no responsibility for any such changes.

Library of Congress Cataloging-in-Publication Data
Names: Mongillo, John F. author
Title: Feeding the world : how innovations in agriculture are saving
the planet / John F Mongillo.
Identifiers: LCCN 2025032838 (print) | LCCN 2025032839 (ebook) | ISBN 9798881807689
hardback | ISBN 9798881807696 epub | ISBN 9798881867591 adobe pdf
Subjects: LCSH: Food security—Climatic factors | Sustainable agriculture |
Climate change adaptation | Alternative agriculture
Classification: LCC HD9000.5 .M665 2026 (print) | LCC HD9000.5 (ebook)
LC record available at https://lccn.loc.gov/2025032838
LC ebook record available at https://lccn.loc.gov/2025032839

ISBN: HB: 979-8-8818-0768-9
ePDF: 979-8-8818-6759-1
eBook: 979-8-8818-0769-6

Typeset by Integra Software Service Pvt. Ltd.
Printed and bound in the United States of America

For product safety related questions contact productsafety@bloomsbury.com.

To find out more about our authors and books visit www.bloomsbury.com
and sign up for our newsletters.

CONTENTS

Acknowledgments vi

Introduction 1

1 Impacts of Climate Change 5

2 Agriculture Production and Global Warming 21

3 Regenerative Agriculture: Farmers Mitigate Climate Change 37

4 Agriculture Technologies: The Future of Farming 51

5 Vertical Farms: Hydroponics and Aeroponics 67

6 Aquaponic Farms, Aquaculture Seaweed, and Floating Farms 85

7 U.S. Urban Farms: Cities Feeding Themselves 101

8 Global Urban Farms: Cities Feeding Themselves 115

9 Agricultural Literacy, Climate Literacy, and Education 127

Conclusion: Agriculture Is Facing Many Challenges 139

Appendix 1: Farm Bureaus, Associations, Administrations, and Businesses 141
Appendix 2: A Condensed History of American Agriculture 1800–2000 147
Notes 150
Selected Bibliography 160
Index 163
About the Author 171

ACKNOWLEDGMENTS

The author wishes to acknowledge and express gratitude for the contribution of government and nongovernment organizations and companies. A special thanks to the following people who contributed resources, photos, and information: Dr. Andrew Smith, Australian Nuclear Science and Technology Organisation (ANSTO); Efraim Lopez, Deputy Air Pollution Control Officer, Mendocino County Air Quality Management District, California; Dr. Liza McDonough, Australian Nuclear Science and Technology Organisation (ANSTO), Groundwater Management, Environmental Scientist/Hydrologist, Lucas Heights, New South Wales, Australia; Jamiah Hargins, founder of Crop Swap Los Angeles and Haley Jones Los Angeles, California; David Ceaser, Lead Agronomist, Agritecture's Daily Light Integral (DLU) Calculator, California; Nona Yehia, cofounder and CEO of Vertical Harvest Farms and Charlotte Hardy, Jackson Hole, Wyoming; the four founders of the Circle Food & Energy Solutions, Valerio Ciotola, Simone Cofini, Lorenzo Garreffa, Thomas Marino, and Alessio Cervellera, Southeast of Rome, Italy; Danielle Andrews, Boston Farms and Greenhouse Manager, The Food Project, Boston Massachusetts; Deni Remsberg, acquisitions editor, Rowman & Littlefield Academic, Bloomsbury Publishing.

My wife, Amy, and family also provided much personal support.

Please note the author is responsible for the accuracy of the content of the book.

INTRODUCTION

Among all ancient human milestones such as the creation of fire, hunting, and pottery making, it was agriculture that ultimately paved the way for the establishment of civilization.
—KRISTINA DEMS, Bright Hub Education

Agriculture is an important industry. But how often do adults and young people think about agriculture? Where does our food come from? Who grows it? How does it get to our table?
According to the World Wildlife Fund,

> Agriculture is one of the world's largest industries. It employs more than one billion people and generates over $1.3 trillion dollars' worth of food annually. Pasture and cropland occupy around 50 percent of the Earth's habitable land and provide habitat and food for a multitude of species. Food drives the world; apart from clean water, access to adequate food is the primary concern for most people on Earth. Agricultural productivity is important not only for a country's balance of trade but the security and health of its population as well.

A *Washington Post* article points out, "For decades, observers in agriculture, nutrition and education have griped that many Americans are basically agriculturally illiterate."[1] That article also outlines a recent study conducted with fourth, fifth, and sixth graders at an urban school in California where researchers found that

 a more than half of them did not know that lettuce and onions are plants,
 b forty percent did not know that hamburgers are made from cows, and
 c thirty percent did not know that cheese is made from milk.

A survey from the U.S. Farmers & Ranchers Alliance found that more than 72 percent of American consumers know nothing or very little about farming and ranching.

Patty McGinnis, Editor, Science Scope, remarked, "Whether or not you live on a farm or in a farming community, agriculture is a topic that is integral to our lives, yet it has been my experience that it is rarely addressed in our schools."[2]

The Role of Modern Agriculture

The term agriculture is derived from the Latin words ager or agri, meaning soil and culture, meaning cultivation. However, today's agriculture is no longer only a soil, water, and growing crops activity. It is much more than that, according to the U.S. Department of Agriculture, National Institute of Food and Agriculture (NIFA). Modern farms and agricultural operations work far differently than those a few decades ago because of advances in the fields of science, bioengineering, technology, and business management. The advances also include more sustainable and regenerative practices to preserve the agricultural environment.

Agriculture can be referred to as an agricultural science (agriscience), a broad multidisciplinary approach in the fields of science, mathematics, engineering, and technology. As an example, one of the fields includes agroecology, the science of managing farms as ecosystems without sacrificing crop productivity.

Other disciplines include plant science and soil sciences, animal husbandry, hydrology, agricultural marketing, fisheries, and aquaculture. Economic and social issues, business management, and sustainability of agricultural farms are also included in the field of agricultural science. Agriscience allows a scientist to delve into a variety of interrelated disciplines to solve problems. Many colleges and universities provide research and career opportunities in agricultural science.

Agriculture and the Economy: A Worldwide Industry

Agriculture is one of the world's largest industries. According to the U.S. Environmental Protection Agency (EPA), in 2024, there were more than 1.8 million farms in the United States.

The Bureau of Economic Analysis reports that agriculture, food, and related industries contributed about $1.537 trillion to U.S. gross domestic product (GDP) in 2023. The sector accounts for about 10 percent of total U.S. employment—more than twenty-two million jobs.

> **DID YOU KNOW?**
> Pasture and cropland occupy more than 40 percent of Earth's habitable land.

INTRODUCTION

According to the World Wildlife Fund (WWF), "Food drives the world. Apart from clean water, access to adequate food is the primary concern for most people on Earth. Agricultural productivity is important not only for a country's balance of trade but the security and health of its population as well."[3]

By 2050, the world's population will be more than 9.5 billion. By that time farmers may be required to almost double the amount of crops that are harvested today. Problem? In the future, growing food and raising livestock with the same amount of land and water reserves we have today will be a challenge. And there are some environmental issues of growing food for the world's population. Floods, wildfires, sea level rise, and droughts impact food production.

However, agriculture is also a contributor to environmental issues.

Agricultural productivity is important. But productivity to feed the world has an environmental cost, too. Agriculture is a major contributor to greenhouse emissions, water pollution, and land degradation. The EPA estimates that agriculture accounted for 10.5 percent of U.S. greenhouse gas emissions in 2022. The two major greenhouse gasses emitted by agricultural activities were nitrous oxide (N_2O) and methane (CH_4).

Worldwide, according to a report released in April 2023 by the UN Intergovernmental Panel on Climate Change, agriculture, forestry, and other land use accounted for 22 percent of global greenhouse emissions, making this sector one of the leaders in triggering global warming.

In 2023, Special Presidential Envoy for Climate John Kerry warned that the world can't tackle climate change without first addressing the agriculture sector's emissions. "This sector needs innovation now more than ever."[4]

Jonathan Patz, M.D., MPH, director of the Global Health Institute at the University of Wisconsin, is an expert on climate change and public health. His view: "It's so important that people recognize that climate change is about our health." As an example, increases in temperatures are linked to more frequent and severe heat stress. The impacts of climate change on agriculture and other food systems can increase rates of malnutrition and foodborne illnesses.

Benjamin Franklin once wrote: "An investment in knowledge pays the best interest."

Knowledge regarding climate and climate change helps all of us to understand the consequences of global warming. We need to be more knowledgeable about some of the fundamentals of climate literacy in a warming world.

In short, a climate-literate person

- understands the essential principles of Earth's climate system,
- knows how to assess scientifically credible information about climate,

- communicates about climate and climate change in a meaningful way, and
- is able to make informed and responsible decisions with regard to actions that may affect climate.

The United Nations stated that "Climate Change is the defining issue of our time and we are at a defining moment." The book, *Feeding the World: How Innovations in Agriculture Are Saving the Planet* provides an excellent introduction for developing a working knowledge of climate-related agricultural issues including challenges in the global food systems.

Individual chapters present a wide variety of people and organizations who are working hard to find salvable projects to curtail the impact of a warming world on the water, air, land, and wildlife environments.

Feeding the World does more than just report about the doom and gloom events of climate change. Yes, the problems are big, but they are solvable. Several chapters provide positive and uplifting topics and the technology to mitigate climate change. The topics include regenerative farming practices, vertical aeroponic and hydroponic farms, aquaponic and seaweed farming, freight container farms, soilless greenhouses, urban farming, and the health issues of farm workers. The AI agriculture technology (agritech) chapters include hardware, software, robots, drones, drip irrigation, and GPS (global positioning system) technology. The book also enhances the text with human-interest interviews with people who heard the call of service.

1
IMPACTS OF CLIMATE CHANGE

Can We Meet Global Food Production by 2050?

By 2050, the world's population will be almost ten billion. A 70 percent increase in food production will be required. The Food and Agriculture Organization (FAO)[1] reports that population growth and diets will challenge farmers to almost double the amount of crops they grow. Even with the doubling of food, hunger and malnutrition issues will still continue, especially in emerging countries.

Increasing food production is not a new topic. In 2011, Tom Vilsack, USDA secretary, reported that the "global population is on the rise and strong economic growth in developing countries is expanding middle classes and increasing demand for agricultural products. We will have to increase food production by 70 percent to feed a global population of more than 9 billion in the next 30 years."[2]

Climate Change Impacts the World's Food Supply

A UN report warns that climate change is putting dire pressure on the ability of humanity to feed itself.[3] Climate change refers to long-term shifts in temperatures and weather patterns caused by greenhouse gases. The gases, such as carbon dioxide, methane, and nitrous oxide trap and retain heat in the atmosphere.

The UN report states that the window to address the threat is closing rapidly. Floods, droughts, sea level rise, wildfires, and other types of extreme weather threaten to disrupt, and over time shrink, the global food supply.

Climate Change: Earth's Running a Fever

The Year 2024: The World's Warmest Year on Record

The planet's ten warmest years since 1850 have all occurred in the past decade, according to scientists at the National Oceanic and Atmospheric Administration (NOAA).[4] In its Fifth Assessment Report, the Intergovernmental Panel on Climate Change (IPCC), a group of 1,300 independent scientific experts from countries all over the world, concluded there's a more than 95 percent probability that human activities over the past fifty years have warmed our planet's climate.

What Is Climate Change?

Climate is what you anticipate; weather is what you get.

Climate change is a long-term change in the average weather patterns that have come to define Earth's local, regional, and global climates.[5] Climate is not the same as weather. Weather describes the short-term state of the conditions of the atmosphere. Weather can change in minutes or hours. However, a change in climate is something that develops over longer periods of decades to centuries.

> **DID YOU KNOW?**
> "If you don't like the weather in New England, just wait a few minutes."—Mark Twain

Climate is the average weather for a particular region and time. The time periods are usually more than thirty years. According to NOAA,[6] every thirty years, climate scientists calculate new averages and statistics. The climate reports include recording and collecting data such as temperatures, rainfall, wind, and other conditions over a large region of Earth and for a longer time period than tracking weather conditions. These events include heat waves, cold spells, storms, floods, droughts, and sea level rise.

> **DID YOU KNOW?**
> In a 2022 survey by the Pew Research Center,[7] 71 percent of Americans said they had experienced at least one heat wave, flood, drought, or wildfire in the past year.

Climatologists Study Climate Change and the Effects on the Biosphere, Where Life Exists

Climatologists are scientists who study the longtime periods in climate history. They are involved in developing computer simulations to predict future climate changes. These changes are based on various factors, such as greenhouse gas emissions. To understand more about past climate patterns, climatologists may also study data from satellite images, tree rings, ocean currents. and ice cores.

> **DID YOU KNOW?**
> Greenhouse gases are shrinking the space available for satellites orbiting Earth.

Ice Cores: Icy Layers Tell Us About Past Climates

Global ice cores provide thousands of years of climate history. Ice cores are cylinders of ice drilled out of an ice sheet or glacier. Most ice core records come from Antarctica and Greenland, and the longest ice cores extend to 3km in depth. The oldest continuous ice core records to date extend 123,000 years in Greenland and 800,000 years in Antarctica.

Ice cores contain information about past temperature, and about many other aspects of the environment. Data from ice cores can provide information about how the concentration of greenhouse gas emissions, such as carbon dioxide, methane, and nitrous oxide have changed over hundreds of years. The icy layers also hold particles—aerosols such as dust, ash, and pollen.[8]

***

Dr. Andrew Smith. Australian Nuclear Science and Technology Organisation (Ansto). Dr. Andrew Smith Researches Ice Cores at Ansto.

Dr. Andrew Smith participated in a National Science Foundation (NSF)–funded expedition in 2013 to Summit, Greenland, led by Dr. Vasilii Petrenko (University of Rochester). This project aimed at improving our understanding of the production of radiocarbon (14C) in the ice sheet by secondary particles produced by the cosmic radiation that constantly showers the Earth. Such an understanding is crucial for interpreting the record of past greenhouse gases, such as carbon dioxide (CO_2) and methane (CH_4), archived in the compacting snow layer, the "firn," and as bubbles in the ice below.

During this expedition, the focus was on the air trapped in the firn layer. The firn cores were returned to Australia, and they are currently undergoing analysis for the record of uranium and other elements they contain that record the use of nuclear technologies from the 1940s onward. The technique of accelerator mass spectrometry (AMS), which relies upon the detection of individual atoms, is used to detect these very subtle signals.

Figure 1.1 This photo was taken at a funded research expedition in Greenland. Courtesy of Dr. Andrew Smith.

***

Climate Change Impacts Growing Crops, Raising Livestock, and Catching Fish

According to the Food and Agriculture Organization of the United Nations (FAO), the past thirty years have seen a rising trend in the events of natural disasters. Rapid climate change conditions continue to impact growing crops, raising livestock, and managing fisheries. The United Nations reported that climate change has affected rainfall patterns causing climate extremes. The climate extremes deliver floods, droughts, sea level rise, and wildfires.

The economy of agriculture, raising livestock, and fisheries is highly dependent on the climate. Any rapid climate change can disrupt food production and availability. The disruptions reduce access to food and affect food quality.

Overall, rapid climate change could make it more challenging to grow crops, raise livestock, and catch fish in the same ways as done in the past.

Droughts and Crop Losses

The following is a review of some of the countries that have faced drought conditions.

United States. Climate change is increasing periods of extreme dryness, particularly in western states. Crops grown in these states are critical for the food supply here and around the world. U.S. farms supply nearly 25 percent of all grains (such as wheat, corn, and rice) on the global market. Changes in temperature, atmospheric carbon dioxide (CO_2), and the frequency and intensity of extreme weather can have significant impacts on crop yields.

The American Farm Bureau Federation assessment puts total crop and rangeland losses from major 2023 disasters at over $21.94 billion.[9] Droughts, excessive heat, and wildfires alone accounted for over $16.59 billion in total crop losses. About $4 billion was linked to excessive precipitation, flooding, and hurricane events. A $1.37 billion loss was caused by hailstorms.

In 2023, close to 80 percent of Texas losses were attributed to widespread drought conditions. More than $4.8 billion in incurred losses was primarily made up of $2.3 billion in damages to cotton, $1.5 billion in damages to forage and rangeland, and $408 million in wheat damage. Kansas ranked second with over $3.04 billion in losses, mainly from drought conditions and hailstorms. Kansas wheat losses totaled over $1 billion, followed by $780 million in soybean losses.

Nebraska's losses totaled more than $1.3 billion, more than $900 million of which was linked to drought. Most specialty crops (such as fruits, vegetables, tree nuts, and medicinal herbs) are more vulnerable to drought than field crops.

Some Major Water Reservoirs Are Below Capacity

Major water reservoirs across the continental United States are experiencing longer, more severe, and more variable periods of low storage than several decades ago. The problems are most severe in the western and central United States. The giant reservoirs of the Colorado River basin, Lakes Mead and Powell, remain far below capacity, Lakes Mead and Powell, which provide the water that forty million Americans depend on, are now only about 35 percent full, according to the National Drought Mitigation Center. Reservoirs on the east coast are doing much better in their water capacities.

Other Countries Impacted by Droughts

Mexico. Approximately 76 percent of the country was experiencing drought through the end of May 2024, according to the North American Drought Monitor (NADM). In 2021, a government climate change group noted that much of Mexico's soil is already considered too dry to cultivate crops and produce food.

The UN Development Programme concluded that climate change in Mexico will mean less rainfall.[10] The lack of water for irrigation will lower yields for grains, such as corn, beans, and wheat. The lack of sufficient crops will also impact food security. Dust storms have caused respiratory and intestinal infections among local communities.

Africa. Many regions in Africa have had their worst droughts in forty years. As a result, several countries including Zambia, Zimbabwe, Somalia, Kenya, and Ethiopia have faced food and water shortages due to drought conditions. According to the International Federation of Red Cross and Red Crescent (IFRC), at least eleven million people are facing food shortages.

Spain. In 2023, reports from the main Spanish Farmers Association stated that drought conditions had affected 60 percent of the Spanish countryside. The long-term drought has caused losses to more than three million hectares (eight million acres) of crops. The lack of water prevented the ability of farmers to irrigate corn, cotton, rice, and sunflowers. In addition to crop failures, ranchers have problems feeding cattle due to dried-up pastures.

India. In February 2024, about 9 percent of India's land area was destroyed by extreme drought conditions. The drought caused crop losses and a scarcity of fresh water for drinking.

***

Climate Change Impacts Glaciers: A Source of Freshwater. Climate change is taking a toll on the six countries of the Caucasus, causing glaciers to shrink and impacting river flows, reports the UN Environment Programme (UNEP).[11] The Caucasus glaciers occupy much of the mountains in Armenia, Azerbaijan, Georgia, regions of the Islamic Republic of Iran, the Russian Federation, and Turkey. The UN report states that the glaciers have retreated an average of 600 meters (650 yards), over the past century. The rising temperatures have caused reduced snow and glacier cover in the mountains. As a result, much freshwater supplies from the glaciers will be diminishing, and the losses will continue to decrease in the coming decades.

***

Floods and Crop Losses

United States. Flood damage to crops occurs when the flooded soils are depleted of oxygen. Most crops grown in North America require oxygen for growth and development. In 2022, floods and flash floods caused nearly 2.8 billion U.S. dollars' worth of property and crop damage across the United States.

Montana. In 2024, President Joseph R. Biden declared a major disaster in the state of Montana following flooding across ten counties in June of that year. Montana's biggest agricultural products are livestock and wheat. Approximately 95 percent of the wheat harvest is shipped across the country and overseas. However, floodwaters damaged wheat, the state's primary crop.

Minnesota. As of the end of June 2024, flooding due to severe storms submerged large areas of farmland. The flooded areas included parts of southern and central Minnesota. Farmers reported that there was much damage to a variety of crops. The crops included corn, soybeans, and wheat.

Iowa and Nebraska. Farmers along the Missouri River lost billions of dollars in grain, livestock, and equipment. One cropland was submerged in up to 3.5 meters (12 feet) of water. More than fifty levees were breached on the Missouri River alone, taking thousands of hectares (acres) out of crop production.

> ### DID YOU KNOW?
> In 2024, farms along the Connecticut River experienced crop losses from flooding.

Overseas Floods

Western Europe. The heavy precipitation in July 2021 led to massive flooding in western European countries. The countries included France, western Germany, the Netherlands, Belgium, and Luxembourg. The flooding caused widespread power outages, road damage, and crop losses in the affected areas.

Libya. In 2023, floods struck the eastern part of the country. More than 4,000 people were killed and some 10,000 were missing. Floods damaged wheat and barley croplands in northeastern Libya.

China. In 2023, floods damaged corn and rice crops in China's northern grain-producing area. Floods may have also reduced rice production in flood-hit areas. Beijing had the heaviest rainfall in 140 years. Hundreds of thousands of hectares (acres) of farmland were flooded. More than twenty people are known to have died, and 1.5 million people were evacuated.

Italy. Emilia-Romagna is a region in northern Italy. The region accounts for a third of Italy's fruit harvest. In 2023, rains and floods swept the region. Several people were killed, and more than 5,000 farms were left underwater.

Pakistan. In 2022, Pakistan received heavy monsoon rains. More than a thousand people were killed or injured, and millions were left homeless. Sugarcane crops, banana orchards, and vegetable fields were submerged in floodwaters. According to local reports, more than 1.5 homes, 63 bridges, and 2600 kilometers (1,600 miles) of roads were destroyed.

Japan. In 2023, record rains in the northern region damaged crops, The crops included rice, soybeans, and other agricultural products. More than 2,000 hectares (5,000 acres) of rice paddies were damaged.

Brazil. In 2023, Brazil recorded heavy rains and floods in the southernmost state, Rio Grande do Sul. The floods were the worst natural disaster to hit the state in forty years, according to CNN's regional affiliate CNN Brazil. About 1,000 people were injured, more than 150 died, and nearly 600,000 were displaced.

Rio Grande do Sul, Brazil, is a major farming industry area. Nearly 3.2 million hectares (eight million acres) were affected by the floods. This land size that is larger than the state of Massachusetts (seven million acres). The expected losses in crop production include corn, soybeans, and rice. The devastating floods are forcing some of the displaced residents to consider leaving their homes in their flooded towns to rebuild on higher ground.

Nigeria. Nigeria is one of the largest populated countries in Africa. More than 230 million people live in this country. In 2024, 300 people died and more than a million were affected by floods in more than thirty states. Hundreds of thousands of hectares (acres) of farmland crops were washed away by the floods. People lost their homes and sources of livelihood. Climate change in Nigeria is evident from temperature increase, droughts, rising sea levels, erosion, and floods.

Climate Impacts Raising Livestock

The production of meat has doubled in the thirty years from 1988 to 2018. Approximately more than 70 percent of people in the world eat meat. Meat products are expected to continue to grow. By 2050, global meat consumption is projected to reach between 460 million and 570 million tons. The top two meat-eating countries in the world are the United States and Australia. Americans consume more than thirty-six million metric tons (thirty-nine million U.S. tons) of meat and poultry annually.

> **DID YOU KNOW?**
> According to the USDA, the average U.S. resident consumes 224.6 pounds of meat products that include beef, pork, broilers, and turkey every year.

Droughts threaten pasture and feed supplies. Dry weather conditions reduce the amount of good-quality forage, such as hay, available to grazing livestock.

Climate change presents challenges for livestock production and health. Livestock health is greatly affected by resulting heat stress. Heat stress problems for livestock include pneumonia and inflammation of the intestines. Increased temperatures can also cause animals to be more vulnerable to ticks, worm infestations, and even diseases. Therefore, earlier springtime temperatures and warmer winter seasons can also be a problem for livestock health.

Climate Change Is Affecting Fisheries

Fish are an essential protein source for more than three billion people. Fish provide 17 percent of the world's animal protein. Fisheries are especially important for some countries that rely solely on fish for much of their daily nutrition.

Warming Waters. Earth's changing climate is affecting life in the oceans. Globally, oceans have absorbed more than 90 percent of the heat from human-caused global warming. According to NASA, 2022 was the ocean's warmest year since modern recordkeeping began in 1955.

Warming oceans can impact many different kinds of species where they live, spawn, and feed. Marine species tend to be highly mobile. Many are moving toward the poles to stay cool as average ocean temperatures rise. The shifts can also cause economic disruptions. As an example, a fish population can migrate out of the range of fishing fleets.

Ocean Acidification. In addition to warming, the world's oceans are gradually becoming more acidic. Ocean acidification is due to increases in atmospheric carbon dioxide (CO_2). As the oceans absorb carbon, the water becomes more acidic. Acidification also threatens many ecosystems. These are the water communities of living organisms that ocean life depends on for survival. As an example, high levels of acidity in the water could harm shell-building animals, such as oysters, by weakening their shells.

NOAA Fisheries works to recover protected marine species while allowing economic and recreational opportunities. The NOAA Fisheries Climate Science Strategy[12] provides climate-related information for fishing industry managers, coastal businesses, and others.

Sea Level Rise Impacts Fisheries and Crop Losses

Sea levels have been rising over the past century, and the rate has increased in recent decades. One major cause of global sea level rise is thermal expansion. This happens when ocean water warms up and expands. The other cause of sea level rise results from the melting of land-based ice. This includes glaciers and ice sheets.

Coastal countries are highly in danger from sea level rise during ocean flooding. The rising waters lead to salt-water invasion. This is caused when coastal floods recede from the land. The water evaporates, leaving the remaining salt to accumulate in the soil. The salty soil causes a decrease in plant growth, lowers crop yields, and results in a reduction of water quality.

The following are some of the countries facing the challenge of sea level rise.

Bangladesh. One of the countries that will confront sea level rise is the People's Republic of Bangladesh. Bangladesh lies east of India. The population is 174 million people.

By 2050, Bangladesh may lose approximately 11 percent of its land. The loss will affect an estimated fifteen million people living in its low-lying coastal region. The rising sea levels are likely to force thousands of coastal farmers in Bangladesh to migrate away. It is also estimated that increased soil salinity, both in coastal and inland areas, may result in a decline in rice yields, thus reducing the income of farmers.

Spain. The Ebro Delta is on the northeastern coast of Spain. This area is one of the largest wetlands along the Mediterranean Sea coast. In the past 150 years, many of the wetlands have been converted into fields of rice. The vast rice crops now cover 20,500 hectares (50,000 acres) of rice fields in the delta. However, the large delta region is vulnerable to sea level rise. The rising waters can affect rice cultivation and production. To prepare for the sea level rise, some farmers are experimenting with strains of rice that can better withstand saltwater invasion.

United States. Sea level rise on U.S. coasts will climb to twenty-five centimeters or more (ten to twelve inches) in the next thirty years. By the end of the century, sea level rise will be ninety centimeters (two feet). These numbers were reported by NOAA and NASA.

The U.S. Geological Survey (USGS)[13] studies report that sea level rise can infiltrate into fresh groundwater supplies. This action can be very problematic to coastal communities. These communities rely on much of their fresh groundwater supplies for their livelihood.

Wildfires Impact Crop Losses

A warming planet and changes in land-use patterns mean more wildfires will scorch large parts of the globe in the coming decades. The wildfires will cause spikes in unhealthy smoke pollution and other problems, according to a UN report released in February 2022.

The western United States, northern Siberia, central India, and eastern Australia already are seeing more wildfires. The likelihood of destructive wildfires globally could increase by a third by 2050 and more than 50 percent by the turn of the century, according to the report from the UN Environment Programme.

United States. In the United States, the fire season is now two, three, or even four months longer than it used to be. Wildfires are increasing in frequency and severity across the western United States. The impact of wildfire smoke causes a reduction in sunlight that reaches croplands. Healthy crops need at least six hours of direct sunlight every day to grow.

California: Wildfires in Los Angeles, California, January 2025. Seven destructive major wildfires in and around Los Angeles have burned more than 22,000 hectares (55,000 acres), leading to the evacuation of nearly 180,000 people. Thousands of people were affected by the fires and the death total reached more than twenty people.

The fires caused the destruction of more than 15,000 buildings (mainly homes). The estimated damage cost will be more than 250 billion dollars.

Many farmers across Southern California also faced the possibility of damage to their crops. The greatest potential impact of wildfire smoke on crop growth and yield comes through the reduction in sunlight that reaches the crop. Ample sunlight is critical for maximizing plant photosynthesis and crop yield. Lower than normal solar radiation can be detrimental. Wildfires damage soil quality, as well. One farmer reported that 50 percent of his avocado crop was lost from the fire's damaging winds.

California: An Earlier Wildfire—The Dixie Fire. In northern California, the Dixie Fire of 2021 was named the second largest wildfire in state history, at that time. The counties included Butte, Plumas, Shasta, Lassen, and Tehama. According to the California Department of Forestry and Fire Protection (CalFire),[14] the wildfire has burned more than 186,000 hectares (463,000 acres) in northern California. Crops and many vineyards were destroyed. The cost to suppress the fire was more than 600 million dollars.

Texas Wildfires. In 2024, the Smokehouse Creek Fire was a record-breaking wildfire affecting northeastern Texas and sections of Oklahoma. The fire is now the largest wildfire recorded in Texas history. More than 485,000 hectares (1.2

million acres) burned beginning in February. The losses include grain destruction in storage bins and more than 10,000 cattle deaths.

Scientists say climate change has made the region much warmer and drier in the past thirty years. The dry weather will continue to make wildfires more frequent and destructive.

The following include some major wildfires overseas.

Australia. For more than one-half of a year, starting before July 2019 and lasting until March 2020, Australia was hit with 15,000 separate fires. Called the Black Summer, the fires destroyed more than seventeen million hectares (forty-six million acres), thirty-three people died, and an estimated one billion animals were killed during that time period. Nearly 80 percent of Australians were affected either directly or indirectly.

Europe Wildfires. In 2022, the wildfire season in Europe was the second worst on record. The European Forest Fire Information System (EFFIS) observed fires in forty-five countries in 2022.[15] These countries were burned by more than 16,000 fires that damaged 1,624,381 hectares (four million acres).

Major outbreaks of wildfires have occurred in Italy, Spain, Turkey, and Greece. The wildfires burn cultivated lands, such as vineyards and olive crops. Wildfires also affected the rural economy and communities of these countries.

Wildfire Smoke Exposure and Outdoor Workers

Outdoor workers, including farm workers, are also subject to the many forest wildfires occurring in the United States and overseas. Wildfire smoke exposure has been tied to a range of serious health outcomes. Wildfires release harmful pollutants into the air. They include fine particulate matter ($PM_{2.5}$). You cannot see these individual pieces with the naked eye.

These fine particles can penetrate deep into the lungs and bloodstream, causing inflammation and breathing problems. Some states, including California, Washington, and Oregon, have taken steps to protect outdoor workers from the dangers of wildfires.

> **DID YOU KNOW?**
> In Peru, wildfires across the nation destroyed crops, but also damaged archaeological treasures sites.

Climate Change Impacts Food Security

The Food and Agriculture Organization (FAO) of the United Nations defines food security as "People having at all times, physical, social and economic access to sufficient, safe and nutritious food which meets their dietary needs and food preferences for an active and healthy life."

The World Business Council for Sustainable Development defines food security similarly to the UN definition. "Food security is the state in which people at all times have physical, social, and economic access to sufficient and nutritious food that meets their dietary needs for a healthy and active life."

> **DID YOU KNOW?**
> *Feeding America* is an organization that has a mission to feed America's hungry through a nationwide network of member food banks to end hunger. Feeding America's 200-member food banks are working in communities across the country. https://www.feedingamerica.org

Food Insecurity

Climate change is affecting all pillars of food security. Increases in the frequency and severity of extreme weather events can disrupt food delivery and availability, reduce access to food markets, and affect food quality. Increasing temperatures can also contribute to spoilage and contamination. Many people lack access to quality, nutritious food.

In a study published in *Nature Food*, the authors found that climate change will impact food security.[16] They reported that climate change will set back farmers' abilities to maintain current harvests.

The number of undernourished people could increase to more than one hundred million by 2050. Honor Eldridge is the head of policy at the Sustainable Food Trust. She reported that more than 220 million people in sub-Saharan Africa do not have enough to eat now. Nearly one in four are undernourished.[17]

Countries in High Risk of Food Insecurity. The United Nations reports that nearly a billion people across the world experience the effects of food insecurity. The countries at risk include six nations in Africa: Cameroon, Burkina Faso, Nigeria, Sudan, South Sudan, and Zimbabwe. The remaining at-risk countries are Afghanistan, Haiti, Yemen, and Venezuela.

Food Insecurity Impacts Health

According to the USDA, Economic Research Service (ERS),[18] food insecurity is associated with ten chronic diseases. Chronic conditions are those that last for a year or more and result in limitations to moving about or functioning. These conditions require ongoing medical treatment. Some of these long-term health conditions include high blood pressure, heart disease, asthma, kidney disease, and obesity.

Adults in low-income, food-insecure conditions are more likely to get chronic diseases. The diseases include heart disease and diabetes. Obesity can also occur when adults and children have little or no access to healthy foods. Obesity can affect physical and mental health.

> **DID YOU KNOW?**
> Childhood obesity is a serious problem in the United States, putting children and adolescents at risk for poor health. For children and adolescents aged two to nineteen years, the prevalence of obesity affects more than fourteen million children and adolescents.

As global temperatures warm, hot days are expected to become more common and severe. Health issues will include the following.

Severe Heat Stress. The impact of extreme heat is linked to more frequent and severe heat stress. The symptoms of heat stress include increased heart rate, rapid breathing, excessive sweating, nausea, and dizziness. However, heatstroke, a serious medical emergency, can occur when the body is unable to control its internal temperature.

Air Quality Respiratory Conditions. A decline in air quality, often occurring with heat waves or wildfires, can lead to breathing problems. The problems can increase respiratory and circulatory diseases. Without reductions in greenhouse gas emissions and atmospheric concentrations, climate change will continue to impact poor air quality. Indoor and outdoor air pollutants have been linked to human respiratory diseases such as heart disease and asthma.

Indoor Air Pollution. Most people in the United States spend about 90 percent of their time indoors. Changes in the outdoor climate can affect the air they breathe indoors. For example, changes in the climate can decrease the quality of the air outdoors. Any outdoor pollutants can spread into indoor environments. These pollutants can enter a building in several ways, including through open doors, windows, and ventilation systems.

Outdoor Air Pollution. Climate-driven changes in weather conditions are expected to increase outdoor air pollutants. These pollutants are ground-level ozone and particulate matter. Exposure to these pollutants leads to health problems, such as respiratory and heart diseases.

2
AGRICULTURE PRODUCTION AND GLOBAL WARMING

Agriculture is the world's largest industry. It employs more than one billion people and generates over 1.3 trillion U.S. dollars of food annually. The United States supplies nearly 25 percent of all grains on the global market. These grains include wheat, corn, and rice.

To produce the needed food, agriculture is also a contributor of air and water pollution, soil degradation, and deforestation in many countries. This chapter will discuss how agriculture production has an effect on global warming, air and water quality, water shortages, land degradation, and deforestation.

> *Washington, May 10, 2023. (Reuters)—"Cutting greenhouse gas emissions from agricultural production is essential to the global fight against climate change," U.S. climate envoy John Kerry reported.*

Special Presidential Envoy for Climate John Kerry warned that the world can't tackle climate change without first addressing the agriculture sector's emissions. "This sector needs innovation now more than ever," Kerry continued. "We're facing record malnutrition at a time when agriculture, more than any other sector, is suffering from the impacts of the climate crisis. And I refuse to call it climate change anymore. It's not changed. It's a crisis."

Kerry reported that agriculture production alone creates 33 percent of the world's total greenhouse gas emissions, arguing that reducing those emissions must be "front and center" in the quest to defeat global warming, during remarks at the Department of Agriculture's AIM for Climate Summit.

The former secretary of state also reported that the so-called climate smart agriculture is a potential solution. The World Bank describes climate smart agriculture (CSA) as an integrated approach to managing landscapes, cropland, livestock, forests, and fisheries that address the interlinked challenges of food security and climate change.[1]

Greenhouse Gas Emissions

The UN Intergovernmental Panel on Climate Change (IPCC) examines how land use changes have contributed to the warming of Earth's atmosphere.[2] Their report has concluded that agriculture and forestry have contributed nearly a quarter of global greenhouse gas emissions. Nitrogen oxides (NOx) and methane (CH_4) are the two major greenhouse gasses emitted by agricultural activities.

> **DID YOU KNOW?**
> Earth's atmosphere is made up of approximately 78 percent nitrogen and 21 percent oxygen.

Nitrogen Oxide (N_2O). Farmers rely much on nitrogen fertilizers. Nitrogen fertilizers are an essential nutrient for agricultural production to sustain food production for billions of people and to keep their soils productive. Farmers add fertilizer to their crops. The fertilizers contain nitrates. The plants use nitrogen to produce chlorophyll, which is essential for growth.

Nitrogen and Human Health Issues: However, synthetic fertilizers are a major cause of fine particulate air pollution. Approximately between 20 percent and 60 percent of the nitrogen applied to agricultural fields is released into the atmosphere. Low levels of nitrogen oxides in the air can irritate your eyes, nose, throat, and lungs. Long-term exposure to high levels of nitrogen dioxide can cause chronic lung disease. Drinking water can also be contaminated by nitrogen oxides.

Methane (CH_4). Methane is the primary contributor to the formation of ground-level ozone, a hazardous air pollutant and greenhouse gas. The agriculture sector is the largest source of anthropogenic (human-made) methane (CH_4) emissions in the United States. One of the major sources of methane emissions is ruminant animals such as cattle, goats, and sheep.

When ruminant animals digest food, they produce methane. How? Look inside a cow's stomach and you will find four chambers. These chambers allow cows and other cattle to eat grass and other plants that humans cannot digest. The animals use a digestive process called enteric fermentation. The fermentation begins when the bacteria inside the animal's stomach breaks down the cellulose in the plant. The stomach ferments it and produces methane as a result. The gas is either exhaled by the animal by belching, or emitted by passing gas and flatulence. During their normal digestion process of the breakdown of food, large amounts of methane are produced.

So how much methane can be emitted by a billion cattle raised for beef and dairy? Author Bill Gates has an answer in his book *How to Avoid a Climate Disaster*: "A billion cattle has the same warming effect as 2 billion tons of carbon dioxide. That is about 4 percent of all global emissions."[3]

> **DID YOU KNOW?**
> Wetlands are the world's largest natural source of methane. The three major kinds of wetlands are marshes, bogs, and swamps. Methane is a greenhouse gas that is more powerful than carbon dioxide at warming the atmosphere. Smaller sources of methane are emitted by natural sources such as volcanoes and even termites.

Besides livestock animals releasing methane gas by burping, manure is another cause of methane emissions. Manure is composed of animal feces and urine. According to the Environmental Protection Agency (EPA), manure waste alone accounts for 12 percent of all agricultural greenhouse gas emissions in the United States.[4] Worldwide, manure waste accounts for 14.5 percent of greenhouse emissions, according to the UN Food and Agriculture Organization.

Livestock animals raised in the United States produce nearly 1.4 billion tons of manure annually, reports USDA's Agricultural Research Service.[5] And according to One Green Planet, the waste is the second largest cause of emissions in agriculture behind enteric fermentation.[6]

Animal waste management practices help to manage manure and other agricultural wastes. The practices are designed to reduce or prevent degradation of the soil and water resources. Storage of manure, especially in large lagoons, also emits methane.

Besides animals releasing methane gases, rice crops can produce methane, too. Rice is a primary source of food for about 50 percent of the world's population. The largest producers and consumers of rice include China and India. The cultivation of the rice takes place in saturated soil and flooded water and contributes to large amounts of methane emissions. On average, farmers need about 1,900 liters (500 gallons) of water to produce one kilogram [two pounds] of rice.

***

The Impact of Air Quality on Farm Workers. It is estimated that 2.4 million farm workers are employed on U.S. farms, according to the Migrant Clinical Network.[7] The number includes migrant, seasonal, year-round, and guest program workers. The workers work seasonally in farm fields, orchards, nurseries, canneries, and fish and seafood plants. Working in the field, farm workers can be exposed to airborne drift of pesticides through residues on equipment, soil, plants, and clothing.

***

Interview

Efraim Lopez is a deputy air pollution control officer for the Mendocino County Air Quality Management District. Lopez's education and working experience include having a master of public health degree from the University of San Francisco and a B.S. in health science from the California State University–Sacramento. Lopez has worked for organizations such as American Lung Association, Sierra Club, California Rural Indian Health Board, and Mendocino County Air Quality Management District. He grew up in a small town in northern California.

How did he become interested in the environment? "In college I began hiking when I could find the time and explored much of California's natural beauty. My favorite subject was always anything science because I enjoyed the lab projects. Nowadays it's mostly the data I'm interested in as a look at large scale population health. I didn't have many mentors. As a first-generation child, I had to figure out education systems, career paths, and industries on my own. What helped me a lot was my people skills and I made friends along the way which created a collaboration everywhere I went."

Lopez says he has "always been an advocate for equity and basic human rights. That includes access to clean air, drinking water, and other rights. Currently I work to ensure that facilities that create air pollution do it in the cleanest way possible using the best available control technologies. Which created the least amount of health concerns for the surrounding environment and its people. The challenge is a balancing act between allowing industry to thrive and foster a robust economy and protecting public health. For example, I would love for the United States to be a world leader in energy but I also don't want to be at the cost of thousands of human lives (directly or indirectly). The benefit is that you know those who absolutely depend on you are now in a much better situation than if you weren't there to protect them. Another challenge is that neither side is happy since you had to broker a middle ground and both blame you."

Lopez recommends that anyone interested in joining the field gets higher education and an MPH (Master of Public Health). "Using science-based data and applying it to real world problems is going to give you all the legitimacy and confidence you need to navigate some of the most uncertain times and varying opinions. This field of broad experience will come with time and willingness to give yourself exposure to challenges. What you will need is the ability to learn. That's right, learn how you learn best, find the method that works for you because it's going to be how you can best understand something in the future. Only once you fully understand the scope and complexities of the issues and challenges can you begin to ask the right questions. That's when the problem solving begins. I feel like I would be doing a disservice if I didn't say this 'need to know' if you are from some kind of disadvantaged community or group you need to know that you can in fact do it. It can become successful in a career and lead organizations to achieve higher education, be published in books. However, you also need to know that it will be more difficult for you to get to that place than other more privileged counterparts. You won't always have a mentor to guide you when you have questions so you will make mistakes. You won't always have financial support so you will have to work your way through school. Therefore you will have less time to study and be more exhausted when you show up to compete in the market. Don't fear, these life experiences will give you an edge once you develop your career. You also have a responsibility to achieve your goals so that you can then help the next generation of people in line who now have you as a mentor," says Lopez.

As to his future plans, he wants to "let the word challenges lead me to where I'm needed in public health. You work yourself out of a job often then you go apply your skills to the next issue or the next step. In my early years I was both a janitor and a farm worker. I worked on onion and tomato fields during the blistering summer heat in northern California. Access to clean drinking water was critical. In some of the earliest years shade and water were not a common commodity, people would suffer from heat stroke, sometimes leading to death.

"At times people think these workers are disposable or even unwelcome but in my experience as someone who has done the work it is incredibly difficult and not many can do it. Most of the time those manual labor workers are there out of necessity. Those positions won't be filled by people who have any other option. That's why most of those farm workers are there in the first place. Now, I am not talking about legal or illegal immigration's what I am trying to get across is that no matter who is doing these jobs it's important to treat them fairly and give them basic worker rights. I was an American citizen and many of my friends were also citizens working alongside migrants and those of us that could (mostly the local citizens) left that work as soon as we could because it was not sustainable. Some rights I am referring to for example are providing water and shade, to give people a fair chance to complete the exhausting work. This way you can develop an experienced workforce so the turnover rate isn't high due to illness. This will protect your crops from rotting in the field because there weren't enough people to harvest. It will ensure a healthy agricultural economy to remain in place because it can provide stability and a predictable workforce. And most important it will keep food on the shelves when you go to the grocery stores.

"An extension of these protections should also include environmental protections. Such as pesticide regulation or developing a warning system for rural farm workers near wildfires. Or protections for exposure to hazardous air quality. When you picture farm workers you don't always picture pregnant women, elderly, or young people in those dangerous environments.

"In this interview, these statements are solely my views and opinions, not on behalf of my current or former positions or affiliated organizations."

Freshwater Resources

The demand for more freshwater is increasing due to the rise in population, economic development, and agriculture production. The present and the future increases in water supplies will put much stress on global freshwater resources. The world's freshwater resources include surface water and groundwater.

Surface Water. Surface water runoff is precipitation that does not infiltrate into the ground or return to the atmosphere. Surface water includes streams, rivers, lakes, wetlands, and reservoirs. Snow that is ten centimeters (four inches) deep contains about the same amount of water as one centimeter (1/3 inch) of rain. Surface water serves many purposes. They include drinking water, irrigation uses, and water use by the thermoelectric-power industry to cool down electricity-generating equipment.

Groundwater. Groundwater is Earth's largest source of freshwater and provides essential drinking water for more than 50 percent of the world's population. In the United States, approximately 50 percent of the people depend on groundwater. Worldwide, much of the groundwater is used in agricultural irrigation.

Groundwater is the water beneath Earth's surface. Groundwater is accessed by means of drilling a well into aquifers. An aquifer is a source of freshwater in an underground layer of porous rock and gravel including sand and silt. Aquifers are a major storehouse of Earth's groundwater. Water above ground level enters an aquifer as rain, snow, or sleet and seeps through the soil. The water can move through the aquifer and resurface through springs and wells.

Ogallala aquifer is the largest source of groundwater in the United States. More than 90 percent of the groundwater pumped from the Ogallala is for agricultural irrigation, The Ogallala Aquifer underlies parts of Colorado, Kansas, Nebraska, New Mexico, Oklahoma, South Dakota, Texas, and Wyoming.

> **DID YOU KNOW?**
> One of the world's largest and deepest aquifers is in Australia.

Water Quality. Water pollution is an increasing global concern reported by the Food and Agriculture Organization of the United Nations (FAO).[8] Water pollution problems damage economic growth and impact the health of billions of people.

Agriculture is a major cause of water pollution and water degradation in the world. In the United States, agriculture pollution is the number one source of contamination in rivers. Streams and lakes. Every time it rains, leftover fertilizers, pesticides, and animal waste from farms and livestock operations can be washed into waterways.

The National Water Quality Assessment (NAWQA) shows that agricultural runoff is the leading cause of water quality that impacts rivers and streams.[9] The runoff of fertilizers can flow into local streams, rivers, and groundwater. Rainfall and snowmelt can also transport these pollutants to flow into surface waters, too.

Surface Water Pollution. Surface water pollution occurs when substances, such as excessive amounts of fertilizers, are washed away from farm fields. The runoff ends up flowing into streams, rivers, lakes, oceans, aquifers, or other bodies of water.

The runoff of excessive amount of nutrients can stimulate algal blooms in lakes, rivers, bays, and estuaries. The algal blooms deplete oxygen in the water. The lack of oxygen is deadly to fish and other organisms. The contaminated water is also a serious threat to freshwater drinking sources, fisheries, and recreational water activities.

The excessive amounts of nitrogen and phosphorus can also travel thousands of miles to coastal areas where the water pollution is formed in massive dead zones in bays and estuaries.

Groundwater Pollution. The groundwater in aquifers is being polluted by nutrients, heavy metals, pesticides, petroleum products, and fertilizers.

According to the Environmental Protection Agency, the pollution of groundwater from fertilizers occurs when groundwater flows its way through the soil.[10] On the way down, it can pick up nitrogen and phosphorus and flow them into the water table. The excess nitrogen and phosphorus can also leach through the soil and into groundwater over time.

The Guardian Report researchers state that 60 percent of the groundwater sources in Pakistan, India, Nepal, and Bangladesh are not drinkable or usable for irrigation.[11] Approximately 85 percent of the total area of Bangladesh has contaminated groundwater. The contaminants include septic waste, landfills, storage tanks, and farming chemicals including fertilizers. Once polluted, an aquifer may be unusable for decades, or even thousands of years.

Other countries that have unsafe drinking water include Uganda, Ethiopia, Nigeria, Cambodia, Nepal, Ghana, Bhutan, Pakistan, Congo, and Mexico.

DID YOU KNOW?

Mexicans are the world's largest consumers of bottled water, both in individual small bottles (1.5 liters or less) and (large, twenty-liter bottles). Nearly three-quarters of people in Mexico drink packaged water, and the country is a world leader in consumption of bottled water per capita.

More than 286 million Americans get their tap water from a community water system using surface water and groundwater aquifers.

Groundwater Depletion. The depletion of aquifers is also becoming a major water crisis. Overuse of aquifers and slow recharge are two major causes of water shortages. Depletion occurs when sustained groundwater pumping is at a faster rate than it can be recharged, causing groundwater depletion. In other words, the amount of water withdrawn (pumped) from an aquifer is greater than the amount of water entering (recharging) the aquifer.

In 2024, more than half of the aquifers in the United States were losing water, according to research published in *Nature*.[12] Groundwater pumped from these aquifers provides nearly 50 percent of the nation's drinking water. If too much water is withdrawn in a large aquifer, the ground surrounding it can sink. As an example, in Mexico City, the underground water table has dropped thirteen to sixteen meters (forty to fifty feet) in some places. As a result, some sections of the city are sinking.

***

Interview

"Groundwater is Earth's largest source of freshwater and provides essential drinking water for more than 50 percent of the world's population," reports Dr. Liza McDonough, environmental scientist/ hydrologist at the Australian Nuclear Science and Technology Organisation (ANSTO).

Dr. Liza McDonough has a bachelor of environmental science degree with honours (UNSW Sydney) and a PhD in hydrochemistry (UNSW Sydney). After completing her undergraduate degree, she worked as an environmental consultant for two years before undertaking her PhD with UNSW Sydney and ANSTO. She now works at ANSTO in the Environmental Research and Technology Group as part of the Water Resources Research project. She has always loved the environment and

Figure 2.1 Dr. Liza McDonough, Australian Nuclear Science and Technology Organisation (ANSTO).

being outdoors, and her favorite subjects at school included environmental science, visual arts, and geology. She says her PhD supervisors were a huge source of knowledge and inspiration, as well as all of the women who have worked with her in STEM roles, although she is continually learning from all of her colleagues, collaborators, and friends.

Dr. McDonough says her main motivation is "the desire to do something good for the world. I also love to learn and understand about how the world around us works. It is a huge source of satisfaction discovering something previously unknown about the environment or an environmental process and knowing that others will be able to build on this understanding through their own research. I also love to train and share any knowledge I have with young scientists. I think one of the challenges we face in environmental science and groundwater research is that there is so much that we don't yet know, and therefore we don't know how our actions and activities are impacting on resources such as groundwater, but also the broader environment. We need more scientists in the field to work in research and improve the management of our environment. The support I receive as a scientist ranges from financial support in the form of income and grants, support with sampling and monitoring during fieldwork from students and colleagues, support from our laboratories who undertake analyses for the researchers, support in the interpretation of dataset from co-authors and support with anything from fieldwork, data analysis, publication writing and more from students and research assistants."

If someone is interested in this field of work, Dr. McDonough advises that "they would probably need some qualifications in Chemistry, Environmental Science or Environmental Management to work in an environmental science role, but the main thing is that you have a passion for looking after the environment. There are so many different roles in environmental research to suit different people. For more practical people who like fieldwork, there are field and lab support positions, for people who like to do lab analysis, there are Laboratory Technician or Instrument Scientist roles, for those who like to undertake research and write papers or reports, there are Research Assistant and Post-doctoral Researcher roles out there. If you have the passion for it, you are suited for this field of work. Environmental research can be quite a small field so identifying people who you would like to mentor you and learn from. Reaching out to those people for advice on how to proceed is a great first step! This could be high school science teachers, university lecturers, authors of publications or anyone else you think might be able to support and mentor you. Because of how interconnected different aspects of the environment is, environmental research is definitely a field where you need to be drawing on the expertise of many different people, so the more people that you are able to get into contact with and draw knowledge and advice from, the better. Regarding where to start, you can start anywhere from researching environmental topics that you are interested in, to volunteering to help with university student projects or fieldwork. Often internships are available at companies and consultancies that allow you to gain some experience and build a network of people around you too."

As to her future plans, Dr. McDonough says that ANTSO "plans on using some of the analytical techniques that are unique to our organization to generate large baseline spatial datasets and maps of groundwater resources that represent current conditions in aquifers. This will provide the groundwork that will allow industry, government, and researchers to build on and move our current understanding of groundwater resources and management forward."

"Two big challenges for groundwater management are climate change and increasing populations. These are affecting both the quantity and the quality of available groundwater. Climate change is leading to more extreme weather events which in some areas is causing problems with a depletion of groundwater resources due to reduced rainfall infiltrating into the ground. In drying areas where groundwater is required for agriculture, industry or human use, it is at risk of being extracted at higher rates than the rate at which the water is now able to be replenished by rain. This is compounded by the need to increase the volume of water extracted to support growing populations, and the increased use of fertilizer, pesticide and antibiotics in agriculture and farming. These contaminants can leach into groundwater causing problems with water quality. I believe we can solve many of these problems through research, innovative technologies, policy changes and the combined involvement of government, industry, agriculture and the public. Our research at ANSTO is contributing to understanding groundwater chemistry and age in various urban, agricultural and natural areas."

***

> **DID YOU KNOW?**
> Presently most homesteads in rural areas of sub-Saharan Africa have no access to piped water. To travel and get water, women and girls can walk as long as two to three hours roundtrip to collect water.

Water Shortages

Worldwide, according to a Smithsonian Magazine report, about 1.2 billion people live in areas plagued by water shortages.[13] They lack enough water to satisfy demand. Considering that the world population will reach more than nine billion in 2050, it is clear that water shortages are a real threat to food security. In 2023, data from the World Resources Institute reported that twenty-five countries, one-quarter of the global population, are facing extremely high water stress each year. The countries are regularly using up almost their entire available water supply. The most water-stressed regions are the Middle East and North Africa, where 83 percent of the population is exposed to extremely high water stress, and South Asia, where 74 percent is exposed. For the Middle East and North Africa, this means 100 percent of the population will live with extremely high water stress by 2050.

Agriculture is the largest water user globally. It accounts for nearly 70 percent of all water used globally, according to the UN World Water Development Report. Inefficient agricultural practices, poor irrigation systems, and excessive groundwater extraction have depleted crucial water sources.[14] The areas where water resource shortages are most severe are in the Middle East countries and those in North Africa. In the United States, depleting groundwater reserves are occurring in Arizona, New Mexico, Colorado, Nebraska, California, and Idaho.

The Colorado River Is Drying Up. Besides the problems of groundwater depletion, rivers are also drying up. The Colorado River in the United States is one example. Scientists have documented how climate change is drying up the Colorado River. The Colorado River system is a major source of fresh water supply for many states in the southwestern United States. Freshwater is needed by forty million people in the cities of Los Angeles, Phoenix, Las Vegas, and Denver.

Is There an End to Freshwater Shortages? A UN report shows that the world is not on track to meet a UN goal: to bring safe water and sanitation to everyone by 2030. By 2050, half the world's population may no longer have safe water.[15]

WaterAid UK reports:[16]

- 844 million people in the world—one in nine—do not have clean water close to home.
- 2.3 billion people in the world—almost one in three—do not have a decent toilet of their own.
- More than 200,000 children under five years old die every year from diarrhea diseases caused by poor water and sanitation.
- Lack of water puts health care workers and patients at higher risk of COVID-19 infection.

***

Agriculture Operations Can Help Protect Watersheds. A watershed is a land area that drains water from rainfall and snowmelt into water bodies. They include creeks, streams, rivers, and reservoirs. Healthy watersheds can provide clean drinking water, productive fisheries, and outdoor recreation. Presently, state governments, conservation groups, educational institutions and nonprofit organizations are taking part in successful efforts to improve water quality in the watersheds.

DID YOU KNOW?
More than two billion people find water scarce for at least one month of the year.

***

Charlene Ren, founder of MyH2O, a Water Testing Network:
Xiaoyuan "Charlene" Ren: Charlene is a Chinese environmental engineer and social entrepreneur.[17] Ren is the founder of MyH2O Water Information Network. The MyH2O data platform is used to test and record the quality of water. The MyH2O is very mobile and an easy way for users to monitor clean water usage. MyH2O data also suggests ways to purify contaminated drinking water.

Ren designed the MyH2O network to provide tens of thousands of villagers in China with data for clean, drinkable water. Her research suggested that about 40 percent of those villagers had concerns about their drinking water. However, they did not have any ability to test it. So, a number of well-trained teams of volunteers went to rural villages with MyH20. The teams conducted water quality field tests, water usage surveys, and clean water demand evaluations. As of fall 2016, water investigations had been conducted in 800+ villages in twenty-three provinces.

Ren is one of seven innovators recognized by the UN Environment Programme. She is a winner of Young Champions of the Earth.

***

Land Degradation

The *National Geographic* reported that more than 75 percent of Earth's land areas are substantially degraded.[18] Heavy rains followed by periods of drought can accelerate land degradation. As a result, the degraded lands have either become deserts, are polluted, or have been deforested. Scientists predict that land degradation will cause disruptions to food supplies.

Much of the degradation has been due to land being converted to agricultural production. Land degradation affects agriculture in many ways. As an example, soil quality decreases through the loss of soil organic matter and nutrient depletion. Nutrient depletion is the loss of supplying nutrients in the soil, necessary for crops to grow and thrive.

In the United States, costs of soil loss and degradation alone are now estimated to be as high as $85 billion every single year, according to the Soil Health Institute.[19] In Europe, agriculture causes 80 percent of the soil degradation.

The Intergovernmental Science-Policy Platform on Biodiversity and Ecosystem Services (IPBES) report finds that land degradation is a major contributor to climate change.[20]

Deforestation

Forests cover nearly one-third of the land area on our planet and are home to most of the world's life on land. They are also essential to human health, purifying water and air. Forests play an important role in maintaining fertility of soil. Forests are also helpful in binding up soil particles with the help of roots of vegetation.

Trees and vegetation provide essential habitat and food for many species. Forest life includes pollinating insects, migratory birds, and small mammals. Forests also provide wildlife with a large variety of different food sources such as grasses and leaves, fungi, nuts, and berries.

In 2022, global deforestation reached more than 6,400,000 hectares (sixteen million acres) of forest, an area bigger than West Virginia, according to the 2023 Forest Declaration Assessment.[21]

The main cause of global deforestation is the conversion of land to produce food such as corn and soy and to raise cattle. As an example, the majority of deforested land in the Amazon is used for cattle grazing and soybean farming. In Indonesia, tropical forests are cut down to grow palm tree plantations. Palm trees provide palm oil for many products; the manufactured products include cosmetics, soap, toothpaste, and food products.

> **DID YOU KNOW?**
> Worldwide, deforestation due to cattle ranching releases 340 million tons of carbon into the atmosphere each year, or 3.4 percent of global greenhouse gas emissions.

Deforestation can destroy habitats and reduce food availability for all kinds of forest-dwelling animals. Several animal species are being threatened by global deforestation. A few of the animals on the list include orangutans, Sumatran rhino, chimpanzees, mountain gorillas, and the giant panda. Some of these animals may adapt by moving to high elevations or latitudes. Others will not.

Forests can act as carbon sinks. Trees absorb carbon dioxide, a greenhouse gas, from the air and enrich the air with oxygen, needed for life. The trees take in carbon dioxide (CO_2), and release oxygen by way of photosynthesis. The carbon is stored in the tree's trunks, branches, leaves, and roots. Planting and conserving forests can help to slow the rate of climate change by removing carbon dioxide in the air.

Forests can help reduce climate change because of the trees' capacity to remove carbon from the atmosphere and to store it in biomass and soils. When forests are cleared or degraded, they can become a source of greenhouse gas (GHG) emissions by releasing that stored carbon. It is estimated that globally, deforestation and forest degradation account for around 11 percent of CO_2 emissions.

Reducing Emissions from Deforestation and Forest Degradation or REDD+

REDD+ is a climate change mitigation solution developed by Parties to the UN Framework Convention on Climate Change (UNFCCC).[22] The aim of UN-REDD+ is to encourage developing countries to contribute to climate change mitigation efforts by reducing greenhouse gas emissions (GHGs), and by slowing, halting, and reversing forest loss and degradation.

REDD+ activities that contribute to mitigation actions in the forest sector and have been globally agreed to:

- conservation of forest-carbon stocks. Forest-carbon stock is the amount of carbon that has been sequestered from the atmosphere and is now stored within the forest ecosystem, and

- sustainable management of forests. Sustainable forest management provides a balance of social, environmental, and economic benefits, to conserve forests now and in the future.

Presently, UN-REDD countries have submitted forest emissions reductions equal to taking 150 million cars off the road for a year.

In summary, where forests have not been degraded, people have more protection from natural disasters such as flooding and landslides. In coastal areas, mangrove trees serve as storm buffers by reducing wind and wave action in shallow coastline communities.

3
REGENERATIVE AGRICULTURE: FARMERS MITIGATE CLIMATE CHANGE

By 2050, the world's population will be more than nine billion. By that time farmers may be required to almost double the amount of crops that are harvested today. Problem? In the future, growing food and raising livestock with the same amount of land and water reserves we have today will be a challenge. And there are some environmental issues of growing food for the world's population.

As mentioned in chapter 1, the subject of increasing global food production is not new. In 2011, Tom Vilsack, USDA secretary, reported that we will have to increase food production by 70 percent to feed a global population of more than nine billion by 2050.[1]

How is our modern-day agriculture ready for the challenge of feeding millions of people presently and those in 2050? Do we have enough fertile land?

If farming continues to produce crops in the traditional way, according to the World Resources Institute, the land needed to grow the crops by 2050 would have to be nearly twice the size of India.[2]

But there are other challenges besides less land to grow crops. A few of these problems facing farmers include climate change, land degradation, water scarcity, droughts, and water and air pollution plus wildfires. All said, the challenges are many.

This chapter will report on how farmers are up to the challenges. They are using a variety of regenerative agriculture land management practices to increase food production. These practices include addressing soil health, minimizing water use, and reducing pollution levels on their farms. Many farmers want to eliminate their dependence on pesticides and artificial fertilizers and provide safe habitats for wildlife.

The Goal of Regenerative Agriculture

We cannot simply think of our survival; each new generation is responsible to ensure the survival of the seventh generation. The prophecy given to us tells us that what we do today will affect the seventh generation and because of this we must bear in mind our responsibility to them today and always.
— Great Law of Peace of the Haudenosaunee
(Six Nations Iroquois Confederacy)

Regenerative agriculture has been adopted by environment-conscious farmers and experts including international organizations.

The goal of regenerative farming is to

- rebuild the fertility of depleted topsoil,
- reduce carbon dioxide levels in the atmosphere,
- prevent fertilizers from polluting rivers and aquifers, reduce livestock emissions, and
- protect biodiversity, the variety of all living things and their interactions.

President Eisenhower once said, "Farming looks mighty easy when your plow is a pencil and you are a thousand miles from the cornfield.[3]" Farming certainly does not look easy, whether or not you see it. Worldwide, farmers work hard each day to produce food to feed the world. And many also protect the farm ecology for the next generation. Their hard work includes embracing agricultural practices that leave the land in better conditions for future generations. Harm has been done, and healing must begin.

Dr. Donald Wyse, Visionary of Regenerative Agriculture (1947–2024)

Dr. Donald Leroy Wyse was the cofounder and codirector of the Forever Green Initiative.[4] Wyse was a professor for fifty years, teaching and doing research at the University of Minnesota. Wyse was the visionary and cofounder of the Forever Green Initiative. It is a model for developing alternative crops and cropping systems. The systems provide longer-living cover on landscape crops. Several of these crops have achieved commercial success. The Forever Green Initiative has gained global recognition and support. Wyse will be remembered for his passion, intellect, sense of humor, and unwavering commitment to creating a better world through agriculture.

***

Jamiah Hargins, Founder of Crop Swap Los Angeles: Regenerative Farmer

Jamiah Hargins uses an innovative solution to urban food insecurity in Los Angeles, California. Hargins describes Crop Swap LA, established in 2018, as a movement of growing food on unused spaces.[5] The empty spaces create green jobs and recycle water. Whether it's a front lawn, backyard, or empty alleyway, microfarms replace the land. Microfarming is a method of farming that involves using small plots of land to grow crops efficiently. Microfarms represent sustainable, space-efficient, and community-centered food production systems.

Hargins utilizes regenerative farming practices to grow food sustainably. The Asante Microfarm is one of the first Crop Swap LA projects. Meaning "thank you" in Swahili, Asante Microfarm grows a variety of garlic, chives, oregano, rainbow chard, eggplant, basil, thyme, romaine and butter lettuces, and cherry tomatoes. No chemicals or pesticides are used. Only organic compost and all-natural animal deterrents are applied. Pond making, rainwater capture, and recycling practices are also established, which use 92 percent less water than traditional lawns. The future plans for Crop Swap LA and how it provides food security for lower-income and often marginalized communities are endless goals to Hargins.

Figure 3.1 Crop Swap LA gardeners checking plants in one of the urban gardens. Courtesy of Crop Swap Los Angeles.

Increasing Soil Health: Carbon Sequestration in Soils

Healthy soils are the foundation of long-term agricultural sustainability. Soil has the potential to serve as a carbon "sink." The sink is a process called soil carbon sequestration. Carbon sequestration is the long-term storage of carbon in oceans, soils, vegetation, especially forests, and geologic formations.

In the process of carbon sequestration, atmospheric carbon dioxide (CO_2) is converted by photosynthesis in plants to organic forms of carbon. About 40 percent of the carbon dioxide gets deposited into the soil. Carbon dioxide is a natural gas fertilizer. The carbon dioxide feeds microorganisms that include bacteria, fungi, protozoa, and nematodes. All of these microorganisms, in return, produce nutrients for the plants.

Farms can support the process of carbon sequestration by increasing plant matter and building soil fertility. In all, composting applications, planting cover crops, and no-till cultivation can improve soil fertility.

No-Till Planting and Conserving Soil Moisture

No-till is not a new concept. It has been a farming practice for several decades. It has gained much momentum as a key soil health practice recommended by the U.S. Department of Agriculture, National Resources Conservation Service.[6]

No-till or zero tillage on a farm refers to a practice where farmers do not use traditional plowing or tillage methods. Traditional plowing or tillage prepares fields for planting and helps prevent weed problems. However, excessive plowing can result in problems. Loosely packed soil can be washed away by water. And sometimes loose soil is blown away by wind. Therefore, reducing how often a field is tilled can cut down on soil erosion from extreme weather conditions.

When farmers use no-till, they do not disturb the soil until the seed is planted. The no-till or reduced till methods involve farmers pressing the seeds directly into undisturbed soil. Any plant material such as old cornstalks and leaves are left on the soil surface. The leftover residue reduces soil erosion, improves water use efficiency, and increases carbon concentrations in the topsoil.

The no-till method can produce high-yielding crops. The crops include wheat, corn, and soybean. No-till practice can decrease herbicide runoff and greatly decrease water usage. The minimized soil disturbance also has the potential to sequester a significant amount of CO_2.

Composting, Mulching, and Cover Crops

Composting. Farmers are addressing the climate crisis by mixing their soil with compost made from farm waste. The composting farm wastes include organic matter. The material includes leaves, stalks, and roots that have decomposed. The decomposed material is added to soil as a fertilizer and to restore the soil, too.

Mulching. Mulching is covering the soil with a layer of leaves, grass clippings, wood chips, and even pieces of cardboard. Farmers are able to reduce soil loss and weeds and increase soil quality. On some farms, mulching has helped increase the length of the growing season.

Composting and mulch applications can improve water conservation by increasing soil organic matter content and soil structure. The two applications lead to improvements in infiltration and water-holding capacity. They reduce water loss by evaporation, giving plants greater access to the available water.

Cover Crops Protect and Build Soil

Cover crops are also called green manure. Green manure are crops grown especially for maintaining soil fertility. Some popular fall-planted cover crops include rye, oats, winter wheat, hairy vetch, and crimson clover. The use of cover crops can reduce nitrate contamination in groundwater. Excessive levels of nitrate in groundwater make water unsuitable as drinking water.

Farmers plant cover crops such as clover or certain grasses during off-season times. This is a period when soils might otherwise be left bare. The cover crops protect and build up soil by preventing erosion. The cover crops also keep the weeds in check. They also reduce the need for herbicides, the weed killers. Cover crops can help prevent erosion and compaction.

The cover crops allow water to more easily soak the soil and improve its water-holding capacity. A 2012 survey of 750 farmers conducted by North Central Sustainable Agriculture Research and Education found that fields planted with cover crops were 11 to 14 percent more productive than conventional fields during years of drought.[7]

Cover crops are a very important practice of regenerative agriculture. Beyond enriching soil health, cover crops play a vital role in watershed protection. Cover crops can provide dense root systems to prevent soil erosion. The cover crops allow rainwater to infiltrate the ground rather than causing runoff. This action not only conserves water but also safeguards water quality by reducing sedimentation. Cover crops have much resistance to plant pests. The plants that are grown near each other are more immune to pests.

> **DID YOU KNOW?**
> Growing crops native to the local climate is another way some farmers are using less water. Crop species that are native to arid regions are naturally drought tolerant. Olives, Armenian cucumbers, tepary beans, and orach are a few of the more drought-tolerant crops.

How Do Regenerative Farmers Grow Crops Today? Many Ways

Multiple Cropping. How can you grow more food on the same land? One option is for farmers to include multiple cropping.

Multiple cropping or multicropping is probably the oldest form of agriculture and is still widespread across the globe. Multiple cropping allows farmers to grow two or more crops on one piece of land during a single growing season or calendar year. By growing two or more crops, the farmer's risk of total loss from drought, diseases, and pests is reduced.

Many farmers grow their corn in a multiple cropping system. Corn can be grown in rotation with other crops in a multiple crop system. They include oats, wheat, barley, soybean, sorghum, alfalfa and clovers, and grasses. Growing a variety of vegetables is less dependent on the use of inorganic fertilizer and pesticides. As an example, the multiple cropping of onions and tomatoes contains marigolds. The farmers add marigolds to help repel some of the tomato pests.

Intercropping: Growing Two or More Crops at the Same Time. Intercropping is the practice of growing two or more crops at the same time in a row. As an example, farmers can plant the main crops such as cabbage, broccoli, peppers, and kale in a row. Then the farmers can squeeze other plants in the same row. Some of the vegetables include onions, carrots, and rutabagas. These plants fit and adapt well in the row. They do not need much space above or below ground to sprout and grow.

Many farmers in the world use intercropping. In the United States, peas are intercropped with barley or oats. In Canada, wheat is intercropped with canola or peas and broccoli. In the tropical Americas, corn or maize is grown with beans and squash. In both Africa and Latin America, beans and peas climb and grow on tall cornstalks. The pumpkins and squash cover the ground below.

There are many advantages to intercropping. Farmers can achieve better weed control by growing two crops. Controlling soil erosion and reducing the chances of soil crust formation is another plus for intercropping.

***

THREE SISTERS: INTERCROPPING IN INDIGENOUS AGRICULTURAL PRACTICES

Three Sisters is an intercropping program planted by numerous indigenous farmers. The farmers are from different regions of North and South America, including the Iroquois and Cherokee farmers.

Why the name? The gardens were called **Three Sisters** because they nurture each other like a family when planted together. And the three crops are inseparable sisters. They can only grow and thrive together. The three plants are corn, beans, and squash. They are all grown together in mounds.

First, corn is planted. Once the corn is several centimeters (inches) tall, the beans are planted at the base of each stalk. The squash is planted nearby. The cornstalk provides a pole for the beans to climb. The beans absorb nitrogen from the air and convert it to nitrates. The nitrates fertilize the soil for the corn and squash. The squash plants shade the soil. Their shadowing on the topsoil reduces evaporation and prevents the growth of weeds. And just like the story, these three plants thrive together better than when they are planted alone. And as older human sisters often do, the sister corn offers the beans much family support.

***

Crop Rotation

Crops are rotated from year to year. Crop rotation is a yearly practice. Crop rotation is the practice of planting different crops in the same field. The benefits help maintain soil organic matter, control pests, conserve nutrients, and protect the soil against erosion.

Crop and pasture rotations can provide an excellent opportunity for farmers to diversify and manage their fields and land sustainably. There are many pluses when crops are rotated from year to year. Rotating crops helps to break up insect life cycles. This practice can decrease the need for insecticides. Some early-planted crops can even provide benefits to other crops that are planted later. As one example, planting alfalfa early in a field provides the soil with nitrogen. The stored-up nitrogen can then assist the future corn crop grow when it is planted later.

The growing of vegetable crops in rotation is an important part of Integrated Pest Management (IPM).[8] The IPM process keeps track of pests very early and their potential damage to crops. By applying IPM in the crop rotation, there is a decrease in the use of pesticides and herbicides on the farm. The benefit of IPM is that it can be used for different forms of pest control. As one example, knowing that a pest may only eat a certain type of plant, a farmer can introduce a new type of plant, depriving the pest of a food source.

Farmers have found another option to cut down on insect damage. They can install row covers. Each row cover is made up of elastic-like flexible material, such as fabric or plastic sheeting. The material can shield plants from pests. The flexible material can protect plants also from the undesirable effects of cold and windy conditions. Once the plants grow larger, the row cover can be removed.

Sack Gardens in Kenya

Kenya is located on the east coast of Africa, bordering the Indian Ocean to the east. The population of the country is fifty-five million. The country of Kenya has many communities that face unreliable seasonal rainfall, and many families have little or not much land to grow food.

However, many Kenyan families are planting vegetable sack gardens. Sack gardening can be done without land. You can find them on family doorsteps, rooftops, and balconies.

A sack garden is a way of growing vegetables in a burlap or plastic sack. The objective is to grow seedlings (not seeds) at the top of the bag and even in holes punctured in the sides. It grows seedlings similar to a tower garden. Looking inside the bag, you will see that the center column of each bag is filled with pebbles and stones. The pebble column is surrounded by soil and compost. Seedlings are planted at the top of the bag and in the punctured holes on the sides.

By pouring water in the pebble column, the water flows all the way from top to bottom and even to the sides of the bag to reach all the plant seedlings. The size of the sack will determine how many plants can be planted in it. In one sack garden, a large-sized bag with 50kg of soil (110 pounds) can grow a variety of vegetables such as beets, carrots, and herbs all year round. Some farmers have found that about eight to ten sacks can provide a household with a regular supply of vegetables. For most vegetables, harvesting is done twice a month.

Farmers Manage Livestock Waste to Reduce Methane Emissions

Methane emissions have decreased from landfills, coal mines, and natural gas systems. Methane is a potent greenhouse gas. However, methane emissions from livestock farming is still a concern. Livestock emissions are from manure and gastroenteric releases. What are some of the common management practices that farmers use to reduce methane emissions?

Better Manure Management. Methane emissions come from "wet" manure management. Wet manure is a mixture of animal waste and organic matter.

Changing how manure is stored and treated can reduce the amount of methane generated on farms. Manure is managed more efficiently by covering it, composting it, and using it as a fertilizer.

Alternative types of feed for livestock. Scientists are also experimenting with alternative types of feed additives. Their objective is to reduce the methane gas produced by livestock. One of a class of feed additives is a red seaweed called *Asparagopsis taxiformis*. The seaweed is native to Australian coastal waters. Researchers have demonstrated that feeding livestock a diet of food containing this seaweed reduced the methane emissions of cows, cattle, sheep, and other gazing animals.

Farmers Conserve Water and Reduce Water Usage

Efficient Irrigation Management

Irrigation is a method of transporting water to crops in order to increase crop production. Farmers can use many ways to conserve water and reduce energy consumption. Besides planting cover crops to conserve water, farmers can use drip irrigation.[9]

Drip Irrigation and Precision Watering

Drip irrigation systems deliver water directly to a plant's roots. This reduces the evaporation that happens with spray watering systems. Drip irrigation provides water-use efficiency more than other irrigation methods. This means that farmers are reducing water usage compared to traditional flooding methods.

Timers can be used to schedule watering for the cooler parts of the day. Scheduling watering use can further reduce water loss. By avoiding overwatering, drip irrigation contributes to healthier plants and more sustainable water use. The main disadvantages of drip irrigation are the high costs to maintain and the fact that the piping can become clogged.

Sand Dams. Sand dams are very effective at conserving water in dry environments.[10] The primary use for sand dams is to provide reliable access to water in dry regions where water is scarce or irregularly available.

A sand dam is a small dam built across a river or streambed. The dam is built to capture and store water in the sand that accumulates behind the dam. Unlike a traditional dam, the construction of a sand dam does not require large amounts of concrete, steel, or other materials. The sand dams are designed to allow the majority of the water in the river to continue to flow downstream. The sand dams help to recharge groundwater by allowing water to seep into the ground behind the dam. This helps replenish underground water sources often depleted in dry regions. Recent years have seen much interest in studies about sand dams as an effective water scarcity adaptation strategy for drylands.

Farmers Plant Buffer Zones to Prevent Pollutants Flowing into Nearby Waterways

Climate-smart agriculture promotes a number of water conservation practices. One water conservation practice includes planting a buffer strip of plants. The plants include shrubs, grasses, bushes, and even trees. The buffer strips are planted between a farm field and a nearby water area such as a pond, stream, or river. The buffer strip acts as an effective protective zone. The zone intercepts and reduces any nutrient runoff of waste and pollutants from flowing into nearby waterways.

Farmers Construct Windbreaks. Fences, bushes, hedges, and trees can prevent gusty winds from blowing away fertile crop soil. These natural windbreaks also have another benefit: they can anchor the soil, reducing the effects of erosion by water.

Rain Gardens

Did you know that there are 12,000 rain gardens located along the boundaries of Puget Sound? Puget Sound is an estuary on the northwestern coast of the state of Washington. The Puget Sound estuary includes salt water from the nearby Pacific Ocean.

Rain gardens are designed to temporarily hold and soak in rainwater runoff that flows from roofs, driveways, patios, or lawns. Compared to a conventional lawn, rain gardens allow for 30 percent more water to soak into the ground.

What does a rain garden look like? Rain gardens vary in size and shape. A rain garden is a bowl-shaped garden of flowers, grasses, shrubs, ferns, and other plants. The low-lying depression of the rain garden allows the collected water to infiltrate into the soil. Rain gardens collect water from several hard surfaces such as rooftops, gutter systems, roads, and sidewalks. The low-lying rain garden keeps heavy storm waters, containing pollutants, from running off and reaching nearby streams, rivers, and ponds. The rain garden helps remove harmful pollutants and allows the contaminants a place to break down naturally. Rain gardens also provide food and shelter for butterflies, songbirds, and other wildlife.

Restoring Wetlands for Water Retention. Regenerative farmers recognize the importance of restoring wetlands. Wetlands act as natural sponges. They absorb excess water during heavy rainfall and slowly release it during drier periods. The wetlands not only prevent flooding downstream but also contribute to recharging groundwater tables.

Agroforestry

Many farmers have adopted agroforestry practices. According to the U.S. Department of Agriculture, "Agroforestry is the intentional combination of agriculture and forestry to create productive and sustainable land use practices."[11]

Agroforestry supplements agricultural practices and protects natural resources. The practices include mixing trees into pastures of growing crops. The trees provide shade and shelter to protect the growing crops and the grazing animals. Agroforestry also supports improved soil health and provides habitats for wildlife. Some of the prominent tree species include poplar and willow species and apple and apricot fruit trees. Agroforestry is very widespread in Southeast Asia, Central America, and South America.

Trees also contribute to mitigating climate change. Trees, of all sizes, are especially good at storing CO_2 removed from the atmosphere by photosynthesis. And the good news is that as the trees grow and get larger they pull more and more carbon out of the atmosphere and store it in their branches, leaves, and trunks.

Reforesting and Planting Trees. Reforestation is a conservation program of planting trees on an area of land to encourage the growth of a new forest. Forests absorb carbon through photosynthesis, helping to reduce greenhouse gases.

Restoring forests by planting more trees protects the land from floods and soil erosion. It also improves the fertility of the land and increases biodiversity. Forests and grassland vegetation bind soil to keep it intact and healthy. Forests provide essential habitat and food for many species, including pollinating insects, migratory birds, and small mammals.

Trees in Towns and Cities. Trees that directly shade buildings decrease demand for air conditioning. Additionally, trees and vegetation can act as a physical barrier to reduce noise and light pollution. Urban parks and forestry can reduce the energy demand of nearby buildings.

Sustainability in Rice Production

Rice is the major food source for more than three billion people in the world. The largest rice producers are China, India, and Indonesia. Brazil is also a major producer of rice.

While rice feeds most of the world, it also uses a large percentage of the world's freshwater. Rice agriculture is also responsible for global methane emissions. However, there are sustainable programs that aim to increase the yield of rice while reducing water requirements and methane emissions.

One program is the System of Rice Intensification, or SRI, an approach to sustainable rice cultivation.[12] Presently, the program is utilized by more than ten million small farms in more than fifty countries. Some of the countries using SRI include China, Brazil, Costa Rica, India, Afghanistan, and Egypt.

The SRI enhances soil fertility and water usage by reducing water requirements. SRI is less dependent on artificial fertilizers, pesticides, herbicides, and other agrochemicals. SRI practices help farmers protect crops against pests and plant disease. All these practices reduce the effects of climate change and greenhouse gas (GHG) emissions.

How does the SRI work? To begin, farmers transplant young, single seedlings, spacing them widely in a grid pattern. The water keeps the soil moist, but not flooded. Nutrients for plant growth include compost and other sources of organic nutrients. Farmers apply regular and early weeding, which allows the weeds in the soil to decompose. In summary, the SRI process provides a major reduction in methane emissions through non-flooded rice paddies. Although more research is needed, evaluations have not shown any offsetting increase in nitrous oxide emissions.

Supporting Farmers' Markets and Local Food

It is estimated that meals in the United States travel an average of 2,400 kilometers (1,500 miles) to get from farm to plate. Food miles contribute to the overall carbon emissions of our food. Trucks, trains, planes, and cargo ships all require fossil fuels to move our food from farm producers to the consumer. However, not all of the food is easily available for some communities.

Farmers' markets help communities that otherwise may not have abundant access to fresh fruits and vegetables. These communities live in food deserts. The U.S. Department of Agriculture (USDA) defines a food desert as a community where residents of the community live more than 1.6 kilometers (one mile) from the nearest grocery store in urban areas or sixteen kilometers (ten miles) from the nearest grocery store in rural areas.[13]

Melinda Cater, a dietitian at Johns Hopkins, helped start a farmers' market in her own neighborhood in 2011. "Produce from local farmers has spent more time on the vine, on the tree or in the ground, so you get better taste and more nutrients," Cater says. "When it comes to fresh fruit and vegetables, the shorter the time and distance from farm to sale, the higher the levels of vitamins and minerals."[14]

4
AGRICULTURE TECHNOLOGIES: THE FUTURE OF FARMING

By 2050, farmers may be required to almost double the amount of crops that are harvested today. Facing these problems, farmers are up to the challenges. They are employing a variety of regenerative agriculture land management practices to increase food production, minimize water usage, and reduce pollution levels on their farms.

Farmers are also using agriculture technology or agritechnology (agritech). The U.S. Department of Agriculture's (USDA's) description of agriculture technology is to include practical technologies to collect data.[1]

Agriculture technology incorporates new developments in agriculture aimed at improving efficiency, profitability, and sustainability of farms. It is efficient in mapping, monitoring, and managing farming decisions precisely. Agriculture technologies come in various forms. They include satellite imagery, temperature and moisture sensors, robotics, drones, aerial images, automation, artificial intelligence, and global positioning system (GPS) technology.

The data collected from these instruments offers information to help farmers regarding soil and water quality, pest control management, and the health conditions of the plants in the fields. These advanced devices allow farm businesses to be more profitable, more efficient, safer, and more environmentally friendly.

The worldwide agriculture technology market was valued at $18.12 billion in 2021. The market is expected to reach $74.03 billion by 2034.

Another Challenge for Farmers. The most recent data shows 41 percent of farmers reported labor shortages in 2018. That's a 27 percent increase from those reporting shortages in 2014. The trend is expected to continue. The Bureau of Labor Statistics projects a 2 percent decline in workers through 2033 despite the number of job openings remaining the same. How can agritech help?

Growing Crops

Farmers invest in technology equipment to collect and analyze data and to manage their farming operations, yearly. The following is a list of some of the agritech equipment farmers are now employing.

Variable Rate Technology (VRT). Variable rate technology uses data and automation to perform a variety of tasks. They include crop protection, applying fertilizers, planting the right number of seeds, and adjusting water irrigation at different rates and in multiple locations in the field.

The VRT setups also allow growers to vary the amount of fertilizer applied through a field. Reviewing soil sample data, farmers can adjust the amount of fertilizer they apply in different areas of the field. Weeds can be more precisely controlled using variable rate applications of herbicides. This practice helps farmers save time and costs by reducing the overall amount of herbicides applied. Variable rate irrigation is another development in VRT. The VRT allows an irrigation system to automatically apply more or less water depending upon the moisture levels at specific field areas.

According to the U.S. Department of Agriculture (USDA), U.S. farmers who used VRT combined with yield mapping had the highest cost savings.[2] The savings was $25 per acre, compared to other agriculture technologies such as guidance systems and soil mapping.

Drone Technology. The agriculture drone market is expected to reach $18.64 billion by 2034. The growth in this market is mainly attributed to the factors such as growing population and rising pressure on the global food supply.

On large farming operations, "walking the fields" has been replaced with drones. Drones are used to scout, map, and survey huge tracts of farmland.

Farmers can benefit from drones in several ways. The farmer no longer has to go out and visually check on a crop. These drones are equipped with special cameras that can visually monitor and record the healthiness of the crop. The drone cameras can measure plant growth. The cameras also provide data as to when the crop will be ready for harvesting. The more advanced drones can carry and deliver payloads like herbicides, fertilizers, and even water.

AeroVironment, Inc. produces unmanned aircraft systems that support growers with precision agriculture.[3] One of the company's products is the Quantix™, built for crop scouting. The Quantix™ can survey up to four hundred acres, (approximately three hundred football fields), on a single forty-five-minute flight. Whether assessing crop growth during key stages, or damage from storm, flood, and fire, Quantix™ Mapper makes it easy to gather accurate images across a large area.

Other examples of drone technology in agriculture include the following.

Monitoring and Data Collection. Drones equipped with cameras and sensors can regularly monitor crop health and soil quality. This data can help farmers make informed decisions about utilizing irrigation and applying fertilization.

Pest Control. Drones can be used to deploy beneficial insects or natural predators to control pests in urban farms. They can also deliver targeted pesticide applications, reducing the need for other pest chemicals.

Water Management. Drones can help manage irrigation by providing data on soil moisture levels. This information can be used to improve water usage and prevent overwatering.

Transportation. Drones can be used to transport small loads of produce or other supplies within local and urban farms or between different parts of the city.

Daily Light Sensors. The amount of light that reaches a plant is important to know because insufficient lighting can result in plant problems. They include stunted growth, leaf discoloration, non-flowering, and non-fruiting. Agritecture's Daily Light Integral (DLI) unit is a tool that allows users to estimate the daily light in any location of Earth. In outdoor lighting, farmers can select which crops to grow, knowing what will grow best in their region based on the amount of light it will receive. Agritecture is an urban agriculture consultant service in New York City.[4]

***

David Ceaser, Lead Agronomist, Agritecture

David Ceaser studied a combined major at the University of California at Santa Cruz of Environmental Studies and Latin American Studies with an emphasis on agroecology. Agroecology means looking at agricultural systems through an ecological lens. Later in life, he went back to school and studied horticulture and business administration. Says Ceasar,

> I have worked many jobs in my life. I have worked at farms in California and in Switzerland. I have sold papayas in Mexico. I have taught kids to garden at schools in California. I have also worked in landscaping and real estate but mostly in projects related to agriculture. I really appreciate the work done by some of my college professors. One in particular, Stephen Gliessman, has done some really interesting and valuable work.[5]

One of his favorite activities as a teenager included gardening. "I remember growing a really large pumpkin when I was young and being very proud of that accomplishment," he says.

> I really enjoy growing plants and trying to understand what makes them grow. So, getting paid to work with plants and answer questions about them is like a dream come true. Working with plants is nice because it teaches you to think about communication in a different way. People will smile or frown at you and that tells you a bit about how they are feeling. We need to observe plants and try to understand what they are communicating to us, which is very interesting to me.

Ceaser says there are many opportunities in agriculture or horticulture.

> Both of these industries are in need of all sorts of people. You can have skills in anything from plant science to advertising and you can find a home in agriculture. Technology is also becoming much more integrated into agriculture so if you are interested in robots or computer programming, you can certainly find a way to apply those skills in agriculture also.

"I believe that urban agriculture is extremely important for several reasons," Ceaser says.

> First, it helps us to understand where food comes from—many people who grow up in cities think food originates in the supermarket. Second, growing food is not easy and seeing and experiencing that challenge helps us to appreciate the extremely hard work done by millions of people to supply us with affordable food on a daily basis. Finally, it wasn't that long ago that almost everyone in society was growing some or all of their own food. It's important that even though we may live in a city, we connect with this part of who we are.

Urban agriculture is growing throughout the world. Controlled environment agriculture is becoming more important as the world experiences less

AGRICULTURE TECHNOLOGIES 55

Figure 4.1 David is very fortunate to get to travel to many interesting locations for his work. This photo was taken at a farm in Jamaica. Courtesy of David Ceasar

stable weather due to climate change. Agritecture will continue to help farmers, cities, and organizations plan for a future where agriculture is more important than ever before.

***

Soil Sensors. Soil moisture sensors can measure or estimate the amount of water in the soil of large crops. By providing the correct water amount, sensors ensure the conditions for plant health. Soil sensors can measure temperature, humidity, and the pH levels of soil. The measurements give farmers a heads-up on soil conditions that may need to be changed to guarantee a healthy crop.

Monnit Corporation is a wireless sensor manufacturing company.[6] The company is located in South Salt Lake, Utah. ALTA® by Monnit Soil Moisture Sensor checks temperature and airflow in enclosures, such as in coops and barns. They monitor photosynthetically radiation (PAR) light in greenhouses to ensure growing conditions are satisfactory. The PAR is the range of wavelengths in the visible light spectrum. The light spectrum is essential for photosynthesis in plants. The sensors can be placed throughout fields and orchards. The sensors can also inform farmers when it is a good time to water their crops.

Agricultural Robots: Good for Farmers, Workers, and the Planet

Sales of agricultural robots are expected to reach 25 billion dollars in 2025.[7] Simply stated, a robot is a machine that resembles a human or other living creature. The robot has the ability of moving unaccompanied and carrying out difficult actions automatically.

Robots play an essential part in present-day agriculture. Robots are the farm machines of choice for many farmers. As an example, low-flying robots can navigate over rows and rows of crops. The robots monitor and collect data on how the plants are growing. All the data is transmitted to the farmers to assist them in reviewing and improving how the plants are growing. Are the crops getting enough sunlight? Do the fields need more irrigation?

Operators can program robots to perform various tasks. As an example, the planting type robots provide greater accuracy to the seed sowing process than manual efforts. Robots can reduce the time and labor required for this task. Robotic automation with vision technology enables crop monitoring at every stage of the plant growth cycle. Here are a few examples.

Spraying and Weeding Robots. Other robotic applications include spraying and weed control. Flying over the crops, the robots can detect weeds growing in the fields. They also can apply herbicides directly on the weed itself and not the plant. This method helps reduce the use of herbicides. This application is a big plus. Each year, 1.3 billion kilograms (three billion pounds) of herbicides are used in agriculture. Therefore, the spraying and weeding robots are a huge plus to reduce the use of herbicides and to protect the ecology of the farm.

Blue River Technology: The LettuceBot Robots. The LettuceBot 1 and 2 use computers and robotic hardware to farm lettuce. The LettuceBot is produced by Blue River Technology, located in Santa Clara, California.[8] Farmers use the LettuceBot video cameras and software to identify and eliminate unwanted buds on the lettuce. Leaving the buds on the plant can result in smaller heads of lettuce with a bitter taste. So, with a squirt of a special concentrated fertilizer, the robot kills the unwanted buds. Using the robot to plant seeds is not a problem. The robots can work to a two-centimeter accuracy. This means that every seed can be placed precisely and mapped.

AGRICULTURE TECHNOLOGIES

"The LettuceBot can produce more lettuce plants than doing it any other way," said Jorge Heraud, the company's cofounder and CEO. John Deere acquired Blue River Technology to create innovative solutions for customers around the world.

Fruit Harvesting Robotics. Today, robots can help harvest strawberries, cucumbers, and even orchard fruit such as apples. The robotic apple-harvesting machine is able to distinguish ripe fruit. In the orchard, the moving harvester rolls along picking just one side of a row of apples at a time.

The extended robotic arm uses a very strong vacuum-like system that picks the fruit. The picked fruit is collected and placed in a storage bin. The bin is attached to the rear of the harvester. In this process there is less handling of the fruit. This machine can pick fruit even at night. Using an apple-harvesting machine can assist the farmers in organizing packaging and processing operations for transporting the fruit.

> **DID YOU KNOW?**
> In the United States, more than seven million tons of apples were picked by hand in 2016.

Global Positioning System. No longer do farmers have to sit in a truck to observe the conditions of their fields. Using the GPS and a smartphone they can follow and keep track of their tractor's exact location and progress. GPS technology includes a group of orbiting satellites that transmit precise signals. The signals allow GPS receivers to calculate and display accurate location, speed, and time information to the user.

The global positioning system is an essential technology in agriculture. GPS allows land, sea, and airborne users to determine their exact location, velocity, and time, twenty-four hours a day. Farmers anywhere in the world can use the GPS technology.

Presently, GPS-based applications are being used for farm planning, field mapping, soil sampling, seed placement, and tractor guidance. Using GPS technology, farmers can now modify their tractors and other farm equipment to automatically run in their fields—no drivers needed. All season long, and in all weather conditions. The GPS also allows farmers to work during low visibility field conditions, such as rain, dust, fog, and even in darkness.

The accuracy of GPS allows farmers to create farm maps with precise hectare (acreage) for field areas and road locations. GPS allows farmers to accurately navigate to specific locations in the field. Year after year, they can collect soil samples or monitor crop conditions. GPS can map pests, insects, and weed infestations in the field. Pest problem areas in crops can be pinpointed and mapped for future management decisions and recommendations. By using GPS on the tractors, the entire process from mapping the field, to planting the seed, to irrigating the crops has been much more efficient than in the past.

NASA Airborne Technology Tools Track Methane Gases. As reported earlier, two of the largest sources of methane emissions is raising livestock and growing rice.

NASA scientists are using several methods to track methane emissions.[9] One tool that NASA uses is the Airborne Visible/InfraRed Imaging Spectrometer—Next Generation (AVIRIS-NG). These instruments, mounted onto research planes, measure light that is reflected off Earth's surface. Methane absorbs some of this reflected light. By measuring the exact wavelengths of light that are absorbed, the AVIRIS-NG instrument can determine the amount of greenhouse gases present. These aircraft and satellite instruments are finding methane rising from oil and gas production, pipelines, refineries, landfills, and animal agriculture. In some cases, these measurements have led to leaks being fixed, including suburban gas leaks and faulty equipment in oil and gas fields.

Raising Livestock

Livestock refers to domesticated animals that are raised for food, fiber, labor, and other products. This includes animals such as cows, pigs, chickens, sheep, and goats, among others. Livestock are an essential part of agriculture and play a significant role in the food production industry.

Livestock can be raised in various ways. They include free-range, intensive, or extensive farming methods. Free-range farming allows animals to graze and roam in open pastures. Intensive farming involves keeping animals confined in smaller spaces to maximize production.

Extensive farming is a method that falls between free-range and intensive farming. In this method animals are allowed to graze and move around in a designated area.

Agritech applications can simplify grazing management of livestock, make accurate predictions, and get the most from their land.

PastureMap by Grassroots Carbon. Grassroots Carbon is located in San Antonio, Texas.[10] The company offers nature-based soil carbon storage solutions

AGRICULTURE TECHNOLOGIES

to companies who want to reduce their carbon impact. Grassroots Carbon partners with ranchers across the United States. Their mission is to help the ranchers get rewarded for storing carbon. Grassroots Carbon matches them with corporate carbon credit buyers.

Grassroots Carbon provides ranchers with PastureMap, a desktop and mobile application for grazing management. Several thousand ranchers worldwide use PastureMap to

- track cattle moves, grazing periods, and rest days;
- calculate stocking and carrying capacity;
- evaluate pasture performance; and
- keep a record of pasture history and plans to move cattle, all in one place.

Carbon Dioxide (CO_2) Removal. How can we control global climate change caused by carbon dioxide (CO_2) emissions? Carbon dioxide remains in the atmosphere longer than the other major heat-trapping gases emitted as a result of human activities.

CO_2 emissions have become a global environmental problem and exposure to carbon dioxide can produce a variety of health effects. Can we remove it from the atmosphere?

Presently, there are several companies that have programs for carbon dioxide removal. Carbon dioxide removal aims to remove carbon dioxide (CO_2) from the atmosphere and store it on land, underground, or in the ocean. One carbon dioxide removal plant is Equatic.

The Equatic company is located in Los Angeles, California. Equatic is building North America's ocean-based carbon dioxide removal plant in Quebec. It will be the largest ocean-based carbon dioxide removal plant in the world.

Using a patented seawater electrolysis process, the plant will remove thousands of tons of carbon dioxide from the atmosphere and produce tons of green hydrogen (GH_2) for electricity and heat. Green hydrogen does not emit polluting gases during combustion or during production. Equatic was named one of *Time* magazine's best inventions of 2023.

Some challenges: There are concerns that tampering with the ocean could impact the marine environment.

Electronic Identification of Animals. Electronic Identification (EID) is the use of a microchip. The microchip can be embedded in a tag in chewed food. It can also be used as an implant to identify a farm animal. Being able to measure the health conditions, behaviors, and performance of each individual animal on a farm is important. But it is only beneficial if those individual animals can be identified easily.

Automated Weighing Systems for Livestock. The information on the weight of farm animals is vital in livestock domestication. Weight is one of the most important indicators of animal health and livestock productivity. Farmers can use periodic manual weighing to monitor the weight of their animals. However, there is another option for weighing. It is an automatic animal weighing system. The animals are weighed continuously and automatically—all done without the animals being disturbed. A weighing system can register up to 3,000 animal measurements per day. The recorded data gives a valid picture of the current situation in a way that would be hard to do with manual weighing.

Water Meters and Feed Intake Sensors. Automated feeding systems can help to ensure that livestock receive the right amount of feed at the right time. Proper feeding leads to better growth rates.

Water meters are used to record information on the feeding and drinking behaviors of farm animals. The information collected can provide an early warning report in case the feeding and drinking habits of animals change. The changes might be due to several factors like disease or unfavorable conditions. When recorded over a period of time, the data also provides a history of expected levels of feed and water intake of the animals.

Imaging Solutions Record Respiration. Using 3D-camera technology and thermal imaging, farmers can study behavioral patterns of livestock. The studies can provide important details of the animals that include lameness, physiological conditions like respiration, temperature, and growth trends.

Fisheries

NOAA Fisheries is exploring how technologies like electronic reporting, electronic monitoring, and other tools can support the need to collect and process fishery-dependent data. NOAA Fisheries is a leader in the use of advanced technologies. The NOAA scientists use a variety of technologies to study the marine environment and the species that call it home.[11]

NOAA Fisheries uses a number of technologies to observe ocean habitats and organisms. The following is a brief overview of NOAA technologies.

Saildrones. Scientists from NOAA's Alaska Fisheries Science Center are using saildrones to study fish like Alaskan pollock and the protected species including whales and seals. A saildrone is an unoccupied autonomous sailing craft that houses a suite of sensors and instruments for collecting data from the environment. Saildrones can be used to study ocean temperature and salinity and record the abundance of fish in a given area.

Researchers use data recorded by drones. The data can be utilized to explore essential habitats. The data can determine the distribution and abundance of species in habitats. This kind of exploration would be difficult to access using traditional survey methods.

Saildrone technology opens up a whole new world of monitoring, recording, and collecting research information. The data gathered may be used to make management decisions about valuable commercial fisheries and conservation efforts for protected species.

Satellite Tags. Tags provide researchers with information about migratory routes; diving, resting and swimming patterns; and internal processes such as digestion.

For example, the tags have been used to track Southern Resident killer whales and where they go and when they leave Puget Sound.

These "smart tags" are especially useful in tracking

- migratory species like sharks, tuna, and albacore;
- sea turtles;
- sea lions and seals; and
- whales, like Southern California gray and Southern Resident killer whales.

Tags provide researchers with information about migratory routes, diving, resting and swimming patterns, and internal physiological processes such as digestion.

Acoustics. Sound is the primary way many marine animals communicate and sense information. For the work of the NOAA Fisheries, acoustic sensing is an excellent way to detect and characterize physical and biological features of ocean areas.

Research Ships. NOAA Fisheries operates a wide assortment of fisheries survey vessels. For example, one of the vessels is the Henry B. Bigelow. Bigelow is a state-of-the-art fisheries survey vessel that is used to study a wide range of marine life and ocean conditions along the U.S. East Coast. The ship's primary mission is to study and monitor fish stocks. The ship also conducts habitat assessments and surveys marine mammal and seabird populations.

Fishing Boats Catch Fish with GPS Devices

Fishers are now able to use GPS devices with fish finder systems to help them catch fish. Technologies include underwater sight and navigation. GPS devices aid in their fishing efforts. Fishers can easily mark an important fishing area so they can return there later. This can save time for the fishers when preparing and planning future expeditions.

Renewable Energy on the Farm

Many farmers are using renewable energy production. This includes photovoltaic solar panels, wind turbines, and geothermal energy. The renewable energy production minimizes use of petroleum-based fertilizers and pesticides. Renewable energy helps reduce dependence on fossil fuel inputs for farming, storage, and transportation of crops. However, wind and solar are very land-intensive technologies with low power densities compared to natural gas. Power density refers to the amount of power that can be harnessed in a given unit of volume, area, or mass.

Wind Energy. Wind energy is not new to farmers. In the mid-1800s to the early 1900s, farmers used wind energy to pump water, grind grain, and cut wood in sawmills. Today farmers use windmills to pump water for irrigation and drinking water as well as to generate electric power to irrigate crops.

Solar Energy: Agrivoltaics. Agrivoltaics is the use of land for both agriculture and solar photovoltaic energy generation. Agrivoltaics is defined as agriculture, such as crop production and livestock grazing, located underneath rows of solar photovoltaic panels. The solar panels are used to power water pumps, lights, and electric fences. The plants growing under the shade of the tall photovoltaic panels are protected from daylight intense sun rays.

From below the panels, the plants, in turn, give off water vapor that helps to cool the tall photovoltaic panels. And on some farms, you can see grazing livestock, mainly sheep, feeding on the native grasses beneath the solar panels.

Geothermal Energy Greenhouses. Greenhouses are one of the most well-known applications of geothermal energy in agriculture. Geothermal energy is the flow of heat energy from Earth's core. Worldwide, more than thirty countries use geothermal energy for agricultural production. Some of the more commonly grown vegetables include lettuce, potatoes, tomatoes, peppers, peas, and sweet corn.

Indoors, greenhouses use geothermal energy to protect plants by keeping them at a proper temperature all year. The year-round temperatures keep the plants from harsh cold and hot weather. Research reports that using geothermal heating for greenhouses decreases fungus infections and reduces fuel costs. Farmers can install underground pipes and transport water for irrigation purposes.

> **DID YOU KNOW?**
> Iceland acquires most of its heating and electricity from geothermal power.

Nanotechnology

Nanotechnology is one of the promising technologies that could improve agricultural productivity through nanofertilizers and the use of efficient herbicides and pesticides. The technology can also improve soil regulation, wastewater management, and disease detection.

What Is Nanotechnology?

Nanotechnology is the ability to observe, measure, manipulate, and manufacture things at the nanometer scale. A nanometer (nm) is an SI (Système International d'Unités) unit of length equal to one-billionth of a meter.

To create a visual image of a nanometer, observe the nail on your little finger. The width of your nail on this finger is about ten million nanometers across. The head of a pin is about a million nanometers wide.

The word "nanotechnology" was coined independently in the 1980s, first by Norio Taniguchi and then by K. Eric Drexler. Many definitions for nanotechnology exist. Most groups use the National Nanotechnology Initiative (NNI) definition.[12] The NNI definition involves all of the following:

- research and technology development at the atomic, molecular, or macromolecular levels, in the length scale of approximately 1 to 100-nanometer range;
- creating and using structures, devices, and systems that have properties and functions because of their small size; and
- ability to control or manipulate on the atomic scale.

Farms

Enhancing Plant Growth and Protection. Nanotechnology offers benefits for agriculture, particularly in enhancing crop protection and plant growth. Nanoparticles improve plant health, fruit size, and yield. For instance, silver nanoparticles help improve crop growth.

Fertilizers. Nanoscale carriers such as clay nanotubes optimize the delivery of fertilizers, reducing environmental impact. Nanofertilizers can control and target release, improving efficiency and reducing environmental impact compared to traditional fertilizers.

Herbicides. Herbicides are the most widely used class of pesticides in the world. Weeds cause significant losses in terms of yield and quality. Researchers are focusing on ways to reduce the use of herbicides altogether. Their research includes using nanoparticles to attack the seed coating of weeds. This action will prevent the seeds from germinating. The researchers report that this approach will destroy the weed even when it is buried in soil. The nanoparticles will also prevent weeds from growing even under the most favorable conditions.

Livestock. Livestock tracking can be a problem for farmers. The USDA envisions the rise of "smart herds" including cows, sheep, and pigs fitted with sensors and locators that can relay data about their health and geographical location to a central computer.[13]

Implanting tracking devices in animals has been initiated for pets, valuable farm animals, or animal wildlife conservation. Injectable microchips are already used in a variety of ways with the aim of improving animal welfare and safety to

- study animal behavior in the wild,
- track meat products back to their source, and
- reunite strays with their human owners.

Scientists at the Kopelman Laboratory at the University of Michigan developed noninvasive nanosensors to test livestock diseases. One of these nanosensors could perhaps be placed in, say, a cow's saliva gland. The sensor can detect single virus particles long before the virus has had a chance to multiply—and long before disease traits are noticeable.

Professor Raoul Kopelman (1933–2023) was among the first scientists to establish the field of nanotechnology. Kopelman was a professor of several science fields, chemistry, physics, and biomedical engineering at the University of Michigan.

Aquaculture

Aquaculture has emerged as one of the world's fastest-growing food industries in recent years, helping to meet the growing demand for animal protein. Aquaculture is the breeding, rearing, and harvesting of fish, shellfish, algae, and other organisms in all types of water environments. Aquaculture is used to produce food and other commercial products.

The use of nanoparticles in aquaculture has shown promise in improving water quality in fish ponds, aquatic animal feeding, drug administration, and disease diagnostics. As one example, nanotechnology provides more effective fish feed for aquaculture species. According to certain research, adding nanoparticles of elements like selenium, iron, and other sources to a fish's diet can help them develop faster.

Agriculture Technology: What's in the Future?

How about growing plants in total darkness? Well, some companies are exploring and testing the possibility of growing plants in the dark. What are some of the pluses?

- lower production costs without lighting fixtures and utility costs;
- reduction of carbon emissions in vertical farms; and
- growing crops, such as potatoes, a vegetable that needs a long duration to harvest. Stay tuned.

The following are some thoughts.

Benefits

Increased profits. Farmers can increase yields and thus profits with the same amount of inputs or achieve an equivalent yield with fewer inputs.

Reduced application of crop inputs. Technologies can reduce the application of crop inputs such as fertilizer, herbicide, fuel, and water. They can also address water scarcity by promoting the efficient use of water in agriculture.

Environmental benefits. Technologies can prevent excessive use of chemicals and nutrients in a field, potentially reducing runoff into soil and waterways.

Challenges

High up-front acquisition costs. Acquisition costs for the latest technologies can be extremely expensive for farmers with limited resources or access to capital.

Farm data sharing and ownership issues. Concerns regarding farm data sharing and ownership can pose obstacles to the widespread use of artificial intelligence in agriculture.

5
VERTICAL FARMS: HYDROPONICS AND AEROPONICS

How does my farm grow? Up to the ceiling.

—*Vertical Farm Advocate*

"Climate change is affecting food production almost everywhere, and the economics of growing and selling produce is affecting everyone," Dickson Despommier, emeritus professor of environmental health sciences at Columbia University, writes. "If we don't do something soon to reduce the rate of climate change, vertical farming may be our last hope of getting food on the table for all those who live in cities."[1]

What Is Vertical Agriculture?

Vertical farming, also called indoor farming or urban agriculture, involves the cultivation of crops in a controlled indoor environment. One advantage of vertical farming is its ability to reduce carbon emissions contributing to climate change.

Agriculture technology (agritech) allows farmers to grow crops vertically. Plants can grow in stacked layers of trays without the need for soil. Hydroponics, aeroponics, and aquaponics technologies deliver nutrients to the plants. The indoor technology also includes artificial lighting, temperature control, and humidity regulation. The primary goal of vertical farming is to grow and harvest the most crops in a limited space.

And the good news: Again, soil is not needed.

Where can you find vertical farms? Everywhere.

Crops are grown in skyscrapers, abandoned warehouses and factories, rooftops, greenhouses, and even inside shipping freight containers. And some farmers grow a variety of plants vertically by employing indoor tower garden growing systems on city rooftops. Fortune Business Insights reports vertical farming market is projected to grow from 6.92 billion U.S. dollars (USD) in 2024 to $50.10 billion by 2032.[2]

Vertical Farming Increases Food Production

According to the U.S. Department of Agriculture (USDA), vertical farming is the predicted answer to the potential food shortage as population increases.[3] The USDA reports that vertical agriculture could help increase food production. Adding more vertical farms can also expand agricultural operations as the world's population is expected to live mostly in urban areas, reported by the United Nations. Vertical farms use soilless technology. Yes. No soil?

The keys to plant growth include a variety of mineral nutrients. The three main nutrients are nitrogen (N), phosphorus (P), and potassium (K). The other minerals include calcium (Ca), copper (Cu), and zinc (Zn). All plants require essential nutrients to grow and reproduce. But do they need the soil to grow? Yes, but. The soil also acts as a substrate. It is a placeholder, to keep mineral nutrients close to plant roots. Therefore, the soil itself is not always necessary for plant growth. As a result, soilless agriculture technologies use the essential nutrients to grow crops without the soil. The technologies include hydroponics, aeroponics, and aquaponics.

This chapter will report on hydroponic and aeroponic technologies used in vertical farming. Aquaponics and aquaculture are featured in chapter 6.

Hydroponics

Hydroponic farming has a history. The Aztecs used a similar practice, called chinampas, by growing the hanging roots of plants on rafts floating above rivers and lakes.

Dr. William F. Gericke (1882–1970) of the University of California coined the term "hydroponics," a word derived from the Greek words *hydro*, meaning water, and *ponos* meaning labor, or "water-working." His work is the basis for modern hydroponic growth in hydroponic gardening. To grow plants, water delivers a nutrient-rich solution to the plant roots. The benefits include faster growth cycles and increased yields.

Hydroponics is the process of growing plants in a liquid nutrient solution without soil. The plant roots are submerged in a solution of nutrients. The growth

VERTICAL FARMS

rate of a hydroponic plant can be 30 to 50 percent faster than plants growing in outdoor soil. Some of the hydroponic crops include lettuce, radishes, carrots, kale, and other leafy greens.

Besides no soil, the benefits of hydroponics include less water consumption, no weeds, and fewer if any pesticides. Very little space is required to grow plants all year long.

According to one hydroponics global market report in 2024, the hydroponics market size has grown rapidly in recent years. It grew from $14.12 billion in 2023 to $15.69 billion in 2024.[4]

> **DID YOU KNOW?**
> More history: The history of hydroponics dates to the famed Hanging Gardens of Babylon, one of the Seven Wonders of the Ancient World. About 600 B.C. the famous Hanging Gardens of Babylon are largely believed to have functioned according to hydroponic principles used to grow trees, shrubs, and vines.

In the United States, as of 2024, there were more than 3,000 hydroponic businesses. This is one story.

***

Interview

Vertical Harvest Farms, Jackson Hole, Wyoming. Nona Yehia is the cofounder and CEO. In 2020, Nona was chosen for a CNN Champions for Change Award.[5] The award profiles ten innovators leading the charge to a better world with new ideas and groundbreaking solutions.

"Vertical Harvest is a hydroponic indoor farming company building a national network of local farms, rooted in the belief that food systems can be both sustainable and inclusive. We grow fresh, high-quality produce while pioneering customized employment for people with disabilities, demonstrating that a more equitable future is also a more abundant one. For us, 'good' isn't just a value—it's a flavor, a mission, and a movement."

Yehia studied at the University of Michigan for her undergraduate degree and later earned her graduate degree from Columbia University.

Figure 5.1 Nona Yehia, cofounder and CEO of Vertical Harvest Farms. Courtesy of Vertical Harvest Farms.

In New York City, she worked for the groundbreaking architecture firm Reiser + Umemoto, where she explored how design can be a powerful vehicle for change at all scales. Her career has been rooted in understanding how communities are shaped—the fabric and infrastructure that make them successful, where they support people, and, more importantly, where they fall short.

Through this work, Yehia came to understand that "food is one of the strongest connections between human and environmental health. This realization led me to explore how we could design a farm that was also a building—one that would bolster the local food economy at scale and create an enduring piece of infrastructure with lasting value. An architect by training and a partner at GYDE Architects in Jackson, Wyoming, I have been working to bring Vertical Harvest to life since 2010. I led the launch of the company's pilot farm in Jackson in 2016 and now spearhead

Figure 5.2 Vertical Harvest employee Tim McLaurin and his job support, Pete Estay, carrying VH produce boxes for delivery to local restaurants. Courtesy of Vertical Harvest Farms

its expansion, with our next-generation vertical farm set to open in Westbrook, Maine, just outside of Portland."

Yehia was born in Detroit, Michigan, the daughter of Lebanese immigrants who had come to the United States to build a new future. "My father had been recruited to do his residency at Henry Ford Hospital, and together with my mother, they embraced this new chapter. But in 1975, when I was four, my family made the decision to return to Lebanon. Just a week after we arrived, the Lebanese Civil War erupted. For a year and a half, we lived through the conflict, navigating a world suddenly shaped by uncertainty and instability. Eventually, my parents made the difficult decision to leave again, returning to the United States and settling back in the Detroit area, where I would spend the rest of my childhood. From third grade on, I attended University Liggett School, where I developed a deep curiosity about the world around me—how things were built, how spaces shaped experience, and how environments could either empower or constrain people's lives.

"That curiosity led me to the University of Michigan, where I discovered architecture—a field that combined creativity, problem-solving, and the potential to create lasting impact. I pursued that passion further, earning my master's degree at Columbia University, where I began to explore how design could be a tool for transformation at both the human and environmental scale," says Yehia.

She continues that growing up with a brother with disabilities "shaped so much of who I am. It wasn't always easy—he needed a lot of attention, and I often felt like I had to step up in ways that most kids my age didn't. But without even realizing it, I became an advocate before I knew what the word meant. I saw, firsthand, how the systems in our community weren't designed to serve him the way they served me. That awareness stuck with me and shaped the way I saw the world. Music became one of the most powerful ways we connected. It was something that leveled the playing field between us, something we could enjoy together without barriers. I used to organize concerts to benefit his school, where I played DJ and he took center stage, singing karaoke-style to an audience that cheered us on—whether we were any good or not didn't seem to matter. What mattered was the pure joy of it, the way music brought us, and everyone around us, together. That love for music stayed with me. I was drawn to independent music and radio, fascinated by the way sound could tell a story, build a movement, and create community. At the same time, I found another creative outlet in painting and art—ways to express what I was feeling when words weren't enough. Looking back, everything I loved was about connection, expression, and creating space for people to feel seen. Inclusivity and accessibility weren't just ideas I believed in; they were something I lived, even before I had the language for it."

Throughout Yehia's studies and career, she says "I've been fortunate to learn from incredible mentors who have shaped my thinking and my path. One of the most influential was Dickson Despommier, whose pioneering work in vertical farming helped me see the intersection of architecture, sustainability, and food in a completely new way. His vision for growing food in cities—inside buildings instead of on traditional farmland—challenged conventional ideas and inspired me to explore how design could support not just structures, but ecosystems of people, food, and opportunity. Beyond the academic world, my mentors have been those who helped me understand how design can drive real change. Working at Reiser + Umemoto, I was exposed to architecture as a tool for transformation—how the built environment influences communities, economies, and the ways people interact with the world around them. That experience reinforced my belief that design isn't just about aesthetics; it's about impact."

Then, she notes, there were the unexpected mentors: "colleagues, farmers, and advocates who deepened my understanding of food systems, labor, and inclusion. The individuals I've worked alongside at Vertical Harvest have taught me just as much as the professors and architects who shaped my early career. Their lived experiences have been some of my most valuable lessons, pushing me to think beyond conventional structures and to build systems that work for people who are often overlooked. Each of these mentors helped me refine my vision. They reinforced that meaningful change happens at the intersection of disciplines, where ideas collide and evolve into something bigger than any one person's perspective."

Yehia says she's always been "fascinated by the way systems, space, and place shape communities—how the built environment can either empower people or leave them behind. That understanding has been one of the strongest motivators in my design approach. I've never been interested in design for design's sake; I'm driven by the idea that we can create solutions that address multiple challenges at once, shaping spaces that don't just function but actively support the people who use them.

"Seeing the impact of Vertical Harvest's pilot farm in Jackson reinforced that belief. What started as an idea—creating a farm that was also a building—became a living, breathing part of the community. It proved that design can be both elegant and deeply functional, that a single piece of infrastructure can simultaneously strengthen the local food system, provide meaningful jobs, and contribute to the social and economic fabric of a place. But building something truly innovative is never easy. One of the biggest challenges is pushing against systems that weren't built for this kind of thinking—whether that's outdated policies, traditional funding models, or even the skepticism that comes with doing something differently. There's also the complexity of designing for both efficiency and inclusion. A vertical farm needs to function at a high level agriculturally and economically, but it also has to be a place where people of all abilities can thrive. Balancing those priorities takes constant iteration and problem solving.

"The rewards, though, far outweigh the challenges. The most fulfilling moments come from seeing how these spaces change lives—watching someone find purpose in a job designed to support their strengths, seeing fresh food grown in the heart of a city reach local tables, and knowing that we're proving a new model is possible. It's not just about the farm—it's about what it represents: the idea that communities can be built differently, that inclusion can be a foundation rather than an afterthought, and that design has the power to create lasting change."

According to Yehia, at Vertical Harvest, "our farms don't just grow food—they cultivate opportunity. Our Grow Well model is the foundation of that mission, a proprietary approach to customized employment designed for individuals who have historically faced barriers to meaningful work. This is especially critical for people with disabilities, who are unemployed at twice the rate of the general population. But we believe that work should be accessible to everyone, and more than that—it should be enriching, purposeful, and empowering. Grow Well is more than just a hiring strategy; it's a dynamic framework that reimagines what an inclusive workforce can look like. We focus on on-the-job customizations and accommodations, ensuring that each role is tailored to an individual's strengths while providing the tools and support they need to succeed. Our workforce development programs equip employees with transferable skills, opening doors to broader career opportunities. And through wraparound services, we help employees navigate not just their jobs, but also the social and logistical barriers that can impact long-term success. A core part of our approach is Competitive Integrated Employment, ensuring that individuals with disabilities work alongside their peers in a fully inclusive environment, earning the same wages and opportunities for advancement as anyone else. But Grow Well goes beyond employment; it's rooted in the seven dimensions of wellness, a philosophy that acknowledges that success at work is deeply connected to a person's overall well-being. From mental and physical health to social connection and financial stability, we recognize that our employees thrive when they are supported as whole people."

Yehia continues that "in many ways, if the farm is the door to a more sustainable and equitable future of food, then Grow Well is the key that unlocks it. It ensures that our farms are more than just places of production—they are places of empowerment, resilience, and opportunity, where every individual, regardless of ability, can contribute, grow, and be valued."

What advice would Yehia give individuals just starting out in the field? "The world of indoor farming—especially vertical farming—is still in its early days. It's an industry that's evolving in real-time, which means there's no single, well-worn path into it. In fact, with a labor shortage across the sector, we like to say come one, come all. We don't expect anyone to arrive with all the answers. Controlled environment agriculture is a brave new world, and even those of us who have been in it for years are constantly learning and adapting. That's why mindset and attitude matter more to us than a résumé full of specific experiences. Curiosity, adaptability, and a willingness to problem-solve are what makes someone successful in this field.

"Of course, we welcome people with backgrounds in farming, plant biology, advanced systems, and technology, but very few come to us knowing everything they need on day one. This is an industry that requires on-the-job learning, creative thinking, and collaboration. If you're interested in this field, the best preparation isn't just technical—it's about being open to innovation, embracing challenges, and seeing opportunities where others might see obstacles. So for young people who are excited about vertical farming, my advice is simple: be ready to learn, be ready to build, and be ready to rethink what's possible."

Looking to the future, Vertical Farms is on the cusp of an exciting new chapter as Yehia says they are preparing to open their next farm in Westbrook, Maine in 2025. "This expansion isn't just about scaling our operations—it's about deepening our role in the regional food system. We're proud to contribute to the New England Food Vision, which aims to produce 30 percent of the region's food locally by 2030. With our farm set to put out 2.7 million pounds of fresh produce annually, we know we'll be making a meaningful impact on food security, sustainability, and economic resilience in the region. But our vision extends far beyond production numbers. We see our farms as essential climate adaptations in a world where traditional agriculture is increasingly vulnerable to water stress, extreme weather, and other systemic shocks. Vertical farming isn't just a way to grow food—it's a way to future-proof our ability to feed ourselves.

"At the heart of it all, our mission remains the same: to build a more sustainable and inclusive food system. We aren't just growing crops; we're growing opportunity, equity, and resilience. This is more than a business— it's a movement, one that we believe will continue shaping communities and food systems for decades to come."

***

Many countries in the world have vertical gardens. The following are a few of the major ones.

United Arab Emirates (UAE). Bustanica, meaning your garden or orchard in Arabic, is the world's largest vertical farm. The facility is the first for Emirates Crop One (ECO1). The facility is a joint venture between Emirates Flight Catering (EKFC) and Crop One. Crop One is an industry leader in technology-driven indoor vertical farming. The Bustanica farm is located in Dubai, a city of more than three million people.

Bustanica is located inside a three-floor warehouse-like building near the Dubai International Airport. The area of the vertical farm would be the size of four soccer fields.

Looking inside the facility, you will see stacks of shelves with trays going up to the ceiling. Each tray is loaded with all kinds of vegetables, including lettuce, spinach, arugula, and other plants.

The farm uses hydroponics. The climate-controlled environment allows for year-round, reliable food production. Since all crops are grown indoors, there is virtually no need for pesticides or herbicides. The indoor growing plants are unaffected by adverse outdoor weather conditions and storms. The farm produces 1,000,000 kilograms (two million pounds) of leafy greens per year, using 95 percent less water and no soil.

"Long-term food security and self-sufficiency are vital to the economic growth of any country, and the UAE is no exception. We've specific challenges in our region, given the limitations around arable land and climate. Bustanica ushers in a new era of innovation and investments, which are important steps for sustainable growth and align with our country's well-defined food and water security strategies."[6]

> **DID YOU KNOW?**
> The primary source of freshwater in Dubai is desalinated seawater from the Arabian Gulf. It accounts for 89.9 percent of the city's water supply needs.

Singapore: Sky Greens Vertical Farm. Singapore is one of the most densely populated city-states in the world. With a population of five million, there is very little farmland. About 90 percent of Singapore's food is imported from several countries. One plan is to grow more food by maximizing the land by applying vertical farming technology to grow crops.

Mr. Jack Ng is the inventor and founder of Sky Greens.[7] Sky Greens is a hydraulic driven vertical farm. The farm produces fresh vegetables using not much land, water, or energy resources. All of the plants grow under natural sunlight all year.

Sky Greens' patented vertical farming system consists of rotating tiers of growing troughs mounted on an A-shaped aluminum frame. The frame is nine meters (thirty feet) tall. The frame holds thirty-eight tiers of growing troughs. Hydroponics feed the plants.

When in operation, the troughs rotate around the aluminum frame. This movement ensures that the plants receive uniform sunlight, irrigation, and nutrients as they pass through different points in the structure. Vegetables at Sky Greens can be harvested and packed right where they grow, thus reducing double handling, and lowering cost and wastage.

One of the farm's missions is to provide improved agricultural solutions with minimal impact on land, water, and energy resources through invention and innovation.

Kyoto, Japan: Techno Farm Keihanna. Techno Farm Keihanna is operated by Spread Company, located in Kyoto. Kyoto is the seventh-largest city in Japan. The population is 1.4 million people. The Techno Farm is a large-scale indoor automated vertical farm where plants are grown indoors in stacked layers. The operators utilize special LED lighting in place of sunlight and hydroponics to cultivate crops, all of which are grown without soil, fertilizers, or pesticides. The hydroponic systems use pumps and filters to circulate a nutrient-dense solution that feeds the roots of each plant. The farm recycles more than 90 percent of the water used in cultivation. At full capacity, Techno Farm Keihanna produces thousands of heads of lettuce each day. The farm supplies more than 3,000 stores across Japan.

Chengdu, Sichuan Province, China. China has built a twenty-story robotic vertical farm in Chengdu City. Chengdu is the capital of southwestern China's Sichuan Province.[8] The twenty-story urban farm was built under the management of the Chinese Academy of Agricultural Sciences. The plants grow in upright trays under hundreds of different colored light-emitting diodes (LED) arrays. The robotic farm grows and harvests leafy greens, lettuce, fruits such as strawberries, and edible mushrooms. The vegetables are shipped to supermarkets and restaurants in the Province and Shanghai.

Manitoba, Canada. Opaskwayak Cree First Nation Vertical Farm is in northern Manitoba. Vertical farming has arrived in the Opaskwayak Cree First Nation in Northern Manitoba. The First Nation's goal is to help feed its community and fight diabetes with an expanded vertical farm project. The farm is located inside Opaskwayak's community hall. The farm supplies more than a hundred families in the community with fresh and affordable fruits and vegetables. The Opaskwayak farm employs agritech and computer systems. The technology monitors the health of the plants and checks indoor lighting, the nutrients in the water, and carbon dioxide levels. More than seventy-five plants are grown vertically in stacked layers using a hydroponic vertical farm system.

Container Farms

Many of us have seen a large number of shipping freight containers parked in special places along docks and harbors of major cities. Shipping containers are built to transport goods around the world. However, shipping freight containers can be refurbished to grow food indoors.

Most of the shipping freight containers commonly used for indoor vertical farming are about 12 meters long (40 feet). They are 2.44 meters wide (8 feet) and 2.59 meters high (8 feet 6 inches).The inside space is complete with LED lights and drip-irrigation systems. Vertically stacked shelves are built with trays for growing plants. To keep track of plant growth, special sensor systems are used to monitor water, air quality, and plant nutrients. When finished, it has all of the technology to grow food. A farmer can grow more than one hectare (three to five acres) of food with 97 percent less water than traditional farming.

Today there are shipping freight container farms parked in backyards, vacant city parking lots, and parked at the sides of buildings and warehouses around the world—and even right next to hotels, universities, restaurants, and grocery stores.

The Philippines has one of the most vulnerable agricultural systems in the world, according to Food and Agriculture of the United Nations (FAO). The frequent storms damage crops and disrupt food supply.

The NXTLVL farms, located in the Philippines, are helping to prevent further storm damage to crops. NXTLVL Farms is the pioneer and leading indoor urban farm in the Philippines. The farms grow all of their crops indoors. They grow leafy greens and mushrooms for restaurants and consumers.

The farm uses a typical shipping freight container. The fully enclosed shipping container uses a vertical hydroponic system. The farm's technology systems collect data on growing conditions of the plants. The data includes temperature, humidity, CO_2, pH levels, and nutrient concentration. Farmers analyze and use the data to improve yields, taste, and quality of the leafy greens and other vegetables. NXTLVL Farms is able to provide a consistent supply of fresh produce to their customers, 365 days a year.

The Bahamas consists of 700 islands. Thirty of the islands are inhabited. Nassau is the capital and largest city of the Bahamas. It is located on the island of New Providence.

Eeden Farms is a Bahamian company in Nassau.[9] Eeden Farms currently utilizes recycled shipping containers to grow a variety of lettuces, herbs, radishes, turnips, kale, arugula, and cilantro. Vegetables can be harvested weekly, packaged locally, and delivered immediately to retailers.

DID YOU KNOW?
According to official reports, The Bahamas islands are at risk of losing 80 percent of their landmass by 2100 if sea level continues to rise.

Benefits and Challenges of Container Farms

One of the major benefits of a container farm is that you do not need much land to get started. They are portable and easy to move. Once set up, the container farm can reduce the distance between where food is grown and where it is distributed. However, working inside can be a challenge. The dimensions of storage containers can be a little tight in space for some workers. In some communities, it may be difficult to obtain the necessary permits to allow space for a shipping container.

Hydroponic Greenhouses

Hydroponics is becoming increasingly popular, especially in the United States, Canada, France, Spain, the Netherlands, and Japan. Besides using hydroponics in vertical farms, the technology can also be used in greenhouses.

Gotham Greens, Brooklyn. In 2009, Gotham Greens designed and built its greenhouse in Brooklyn, New York. The company employs hydroponic greenhouses across several U.S. states including Illinois, Rhode Island, and Colorado.

Gotham Greens' greenhouse farms use automated systems to ensure that temperature, humidity, and light levels, as well as air composition, are in exactly the right balance. Gotham Greens farms grow and sell a wide variety of leafy greens and herbs, salad dressings and sauces.

Wellspring Harvest Greenhouse of Springfield, Massachusetts. Wellspring Harvest is the largest urban commercial greenhouse in the state. The greenhouse utilizes the "NFT" or nutrient field technique. In this system, the plants grow in a channel that is fed with a constant stream of nutrient-rich water. After a few weeks in the NFT channels, the results are rich, full-bodied plants that are quickly harvested and retail ready.

Wellspring Harvest grows red and green butter lettuce, red and green sweet crisp, and romaine. The greenhouse's business distributes to residents and supplies several grocery stores between Massachusetts and Rhode Island. Their customers also include local college and university customers.

> **DID YOU KNOW?**
> Disney World has greenhouses on its Epcot property. The greenhouses use hydroponics to produce tons of fruits and vegetables of which much of the food is served in the park's restaurants.

Aeroponics

Richard J. Stoner (1957–2017) is often cited as the father of modern aeroponics. Stoner was a graduate of the University of Michigan–Flint. Stoner majored in both chemistry and biology.

In 1985, Stoner patented the microchip that initially made the automatic watering of aeroponically grown plants possible. Stoner's company was the first company to manufacture, market, and apply aeroponic systems into greenhouses for commercial crop production. This technology launched the aeroponic industry that is marketed worldwide.

Aeroponics is another soilless technology, growing plants without soil. Instead, the roots of the seedlings are suspended in the air and fed with a nutrient-dense mist. This differs from hydroponics, where plant roots are submerged in a solution of water and nutrients—no misting here.

Aeroponics uses 98 percent less land than traditional farming methods. This is accomplished by making use of vertical space as well as horizontal. In aeroponics, the roots have greater access to oxygen. Extra oxygen accelerates nutrient absorption at the root surface. The oxygen surrounds the roots at all times, which results in fast crop growth. Aeroponics also reduces the risk of diseases and pests.

At times, aeroponics is combined with conventional hydroponics. This combination is used as an emergency backup plan for maintaining constant flow of nutrition and water supplies, if the aeroponic system fails.

> **DID YOU KNOW?**
> Aeroponic conditions occur in nature. On tropical islands, such as Hawaii, orchids develop and grow freely in trees. Orchids use their roots to absorb nutrients from the air. including moisture and the carbon dioxide they need to thrive.

Low-Pressure Systems. Low-pressure aeroponic garden units are usually suitable for tabletop growing for home growers. The low-pressure system is a good in demonstration of the principles of aeroponics. In most low-pressure aeroponic gardens, the plant roots are suspended inside a trough. A low-pressure pump delivers a nutrient solution sprayed by jets. Any dripping water then drains back into the reservoir. Many tower gardens use this system.

High-Pressure Systems. High-pressure systems are typically used in the cultivation of high-value crops and plant specimens. Examples of high-value crops include organic vegetables, gourmet herbs, berries, and flowers like orchids. In high-pressure aeroponic techniques, the mist is generated by high-pressure pumps. High-pressure aeroponics systems also include technologies for air and water purification including nutrient sterilization.

NASA and Aeroponics

Plants have been to space since 1960. Experiments aboard the space shuttle and the International Space Station have exposed plants to the effects of microgravity. In 1997, NASA sponsored aeroponic plant studies aboard the Mir Russian space station. Mir was a Russian space station operating in Earth's orbit from 1986 to 2001. The word *Mir* is a Russian word for peace.

U.S. Aeroponic Farms

5 Points Farm, Jacksonville, Florida. 5 Points Farm is an indoor vertical farm in Jacksonville, Florida. The farm features several aeroponic tower gardens with a total planting capacity of more than a thousand plants. Each seedling finds its place in the tower, nestled in a supportive environment that maximizes growth. With their roots suspended in nutrient-rich mist, the plants thrive without the need for soil. The towers utilize minimal space while maximizing crop yield. With precision watering and nutrient distribution, the farm grows healthier, pesticide-free vegetables and herbs all year round.

O'Hare Urban Garden. O'Hare International Airport in Chicago, Illinois has an aeroponic tower garden inside its airport terminal called the Urban Garden. All of the Tower Garden® produce from the O'Hare Urban Garden is hand-delivered to the airport's eateries and the O'Hare Farmers' Market inside the terminal.

LA Urban Farms, Los Angeles. LA Urban Farms uses the Tower Garden® vertical aeroponic food production system. The Tower Garden® technology allows anyone to start a home garden or urban farm practically anywhere, indoors or outdoors. LA Urban farms use aeroponic technology to grow fruits, vegetables, herbs, and edible flowers. All can be grown within twenty to thirty days. The farm uses less water and less land than traditional gardening. LA local urban farms range in size from large commercial greenhouses to rooftop micro-farms.

Aeroponic Farms Overseas

The following is a brief overview of some of the overseas aeroponic farms.

Paris, France: Tower Farm is the largest rooftop tower farm in the world. Tower Farm in Paris features 350 vertical tower gardens located on a rooftop in the city center of Paris.[10] This rooftop tower farm, using Tower Garden® aeroponic technology, grows fruit and vegetables for thousands of office employees working in the building. As one person exclaimed, "It is truly the embodiment of urban farming and vertical farming."

England: Bristol LettUs Grow. LettUs Grow was founded in Bristol, United Kingdom, in 2015 by cofounders Charlie Guy, Jack Farmer, and Ben Crowther.

LettUs Grow is a team of growers, engineers, plant scientists, software developers, and business experts, who all care deeply about food and the environment. Together they design and build aeroponic technology and farm management software for indoor and vertical farms. The farm's aeroponic technology allows plants to grow faster while using less water and fertilizers, and no pesticides. The company believes careful innovation in farming can make the world a better place.

Bergamo, Italy. The first vertical farm using aeroponic towers is in the province of Bergamo, Italy. The northern Italy farm has fifty aeroponic towers in a greenhouse. The towers have a total planting capacity of thousands of plants.

Singapore. Aero-Green Technology is another farm that uses aeroponics to grow crops. Aero-Green Technology is a private company located in the Republic of Singapore. It is the first commercial aeroponics farm in Asia to adapt the aeroponics technology to grow vegetables in Singapore. The 5.3-hectare (13-acre) farm is located at Lim Chu Kang Agrotechnology Park, in Singapore.

Using aeroponics, the young plant roots are suspended and sprayed with a rich nutrient solution. The pesticide-free vegetables include both tropical and temperate vegetables. They include cherry tomatoes, Batavia, Lollo Rossa, and butterhead lettuce, and sweet basil.

The Republic of Singapore has a population of more than five million inhabitants. About 90 percent of the country's food is imported. In 2020 Singapore announced new measures to accelerate local food production. One major reason is that years ago, the coronavirus pandemic disrupted global supply chains. To grow more food, the goal is to modify car parks, rooftops on public housing, and estates into urban farms, by 2030.

What Are the Advantages of Vertical Farming?

Dr. Kai-Shu Ling is a research plant pathologist with the Vegetable Research Laboratory in Charleston, South Carolina.[11] He states: "Vertical farming offers many benefits that traditional farming cannot. For example, the crops produced by traditional farming are limited by geographic region and seasonal changes. Vertical farming allows growers to grow regional or seasonal crops indoors year-round. They can grow crops anywhere a greenhouse or controlled environment can be established. As a result, consumers, especially those in urban areas, who are typically too far from farms and can now have easier access to fresher produce."

What Are the Limitations of Vertical Farming?

Some of the major disadvantages of vertical farming include high initial construction costs, high maintenance of the system, and high level of technical knowhow required. And most important is the high initial investment required for setting the indoor structure and lighting and irrigation systems.

Dr. James Altland is a research horticulturist with the Application Technology Research Unit in Wooster, Ohio.[12] Dr. Altland reports:

"The major disadvantage is that you give up access to the Sun, which is the most abundant (and free) source of energy on Earth. Growing plants vertically in stacked systems often requires artificial light sources, which can become costly. Vertical farming also requires humidity control through expensive and energy-intensive heating, ventilation, and air conditioning (HVAC) systems."

Another limitation is the general lack of knowledge and experience in maximizing crop productivity under a controlled environment. The next and probably the biggest disadvantage of vertical farming compared to field farming is the limited number of crops that can be grown in vertical systems. At this time, rice and wheat cannot be grown profitably in a vertical farm.

In summary, with well-thought-out plans, vertical farming can emerge as a major supplier of leafy greens, berries, herbs, and medicinal crops near urban areas. Advocates believe it has a place in the food system. It can be more sustainable and profitable when planned and operated responsibly.

6
AQUAPONIC FARMS, AQUACULTURE SEAWEED, AND FLOATING FARMS

Aquaponics is the practice of combining aquaculture and hydroponics into one system. Aquaponics is also known as aqua farming. The aquaponic system combines aquaculture (fish farming) with hydroponics (fertilizing plants with nutrient-rich water). All functions take place inside a controlled environment.

For the last decade, aquaponics has become one of the major sustainable farming techniques. Aquaponics has gained popularity among environmental communities. As a result, the aquaponics market is experiencing steady growth.

According to a report by Fortune Business Insights, the global aquaponics market size, valued in U.S. dollar, is projected to continue to grow from $1,145.71 million in 2024 to $2,399.96 million by 2032.[1]

Aquaponic Farms, United States

There are several aquaponic farmers in the United States and other countries. The aquaponic farms are found in a variety of places that include greenhouses, warehouses, and yes, in shipping containers, too!

A small aquaponic system can produce 45 kilograms (100 pounds) of fresh fish and yield 90 kilograms (200 pounds) of fruits and vegetables every six months.

The following is a selection of aquaponics farms in the United States.

Santa Fe, New Mexico: FarmPod, a Shipping Container Aquaponic Farm. "FarmPod is the farm of the future, " says Mike Straight, CEO of FarmPod.[2] The farm is located in New Mexico, where many people live in remote communities. They live far from grocery stores or farmers' markets, resulting in food deserts. According to reports, about 300,000 people in the state, or about 15 percent of the population, lack access to healthy foods.

The FarmPod is a two-story shipping container that can fit in an area the size of one parking space. The container is powered by solar energy and rainwater.

Inside the shipping container, the fish grow in three large freshwater tanks on the first floor. The tanks hold such fish as koi and barramundi, also known as Asian sea bass. These fish are popular in Thai cuisine. As with aquaponic farms, the fish waste in the tanks is pumped up to the greenhouse. The solar greenhouse is on the second floor. Here the water trickles down through the vertical towers. The nutrient-rich water is delivered to the plant roots; the clean water circulates back to the fish tanks below. The farm uses 90 percent less water than traditional farming. FarmPod grows twice as much food in a quarter of the space. FarmPod is powered by solar energy panels and battery storage.

The vegetables that are raised in the FarmPod include herbs, lettuce, strawberries, spinach, collard greens, and arugula. The fish includes tilapia, trout, catfish, and perch.

Brooklyn, New York. Jason Green is CEO and cofounder of Edenworks, an aquaponic farm inside a Brooklyn warehouse.[3] Founded in 2013, Edenworks designs and operates vertical aquaponic farms to produce a range of foods for grocers. Its products include a large variety of leafy greens, such as kale and chard.

The greens grow in vertically stacked shelves. Each shelf contains a series of rafts floating on water holding the leafy greens. The water both fertilizes and irrigates the plants without pesticides or added fertilizer.

All seafood is raised without antibiotics, hormones, mercury, or waste discharge. The farm has several species of fish. The company's mission is to supply fresh products that are sustainable, organic, and inexpensive.

Half Moon Bay, California: Ouroboros Farms. Ouroboros Farms is one of the largest commercial aquaponic farms in the United States.[4] The farm is located in northern California in the coastal town of Half Moon Bay. The farm was founded in 2012 by Jessica Patton and Ken Armstrong.

The fish are given organic feed and are farmed in special connected grow tanks. The fish waste in the tanks becomes the fertilizer for the plants that are raised on special grow mats nearby. The roots of the plant take up the nitrogen from the fish and produce clean water that circulates back into the fish tanks.

The system, says Armstrong, produces mature lettuce more quickly than traditional planting and uses less water, too. The monthly output of thousands of heads of lettuce requires a little less than one liter (two-thirds a gallon) per head.

During the different seasons of the year, the produce includes lettuce and other vegetables such as pac choi, garlic, kale, radishes, collard greens, celery, and watercress.

The farm also hosts training programs and farm tours. The farm consults with new growers looking to run commercial aquaponics operations.

Aquaponic Farms Overseas

The following is a selection of aquaponics farms in other countries.

Rome, Italy: The Circle Food & Energy Solutions. The Circle Food & Energy Solutions aquaponic farm is located southeast of Rome, Italy.[5] The Circle Food & Energy Solutions is a farm designed to produce food and use energy in the most sustainable and competitive way through aquaponics.

The Circle farm has a huge tank that holds Japanese koi fish. Koi are a type of carp, a common freshwater fish that can be found all over the world. The koi fish naturally fertilizes the farm plants, and in turn the plants purify the water.

***

Interview

The Circle Food & Energy Solutions Aquaponic Farm is in Via del Casale Ciminelli, Rome, Italy. The founders of The Circle have an innovative agricultural specializing in aquaponics. The founders include:

Valerio Ciotola: cofounder, president, and chief scientist

Thomas Marino: cofounder, director of strategy, marketing, and sales

Simone Cofini: cofounder, director of plant engineering and technological development

Lorenzo Garreffa: cofounder, production director and head of the lab

The backgrounds of all of the founders are rooted in different fields that complement each other. Valerio, Simone, and Lorenzo have doctorates in biotechnology, while Thomas has a background in political science and business strategy. This interdisciplinary knowledge has been crucial in developing the Circle's innovative approach to sustainable food production.

"We were driven by the urgent need to create a sustainable and efficient food production model that could address modern environmental challenges," the founders say. "Traditional agriculture consumes vast

Figure 6.1 The Founders of The Circle Food & Energy Solutions Aquaponic Farm. Courtesy of the Circle Food and Energy Solutions.

Figure 6.2 The farm grows various types of baby leaf greens and aromatic herbs. Each tower can accommodate dozens of plants, and the facility hosts hundreds of these towers, cultivating more than 90,000 plants in total. Courtesy of the Circle Food and Energy Solutions.

AQUAPONIC FARMS, AQUACULTURE SEAWEED, AND FLOATING FARMS

Figure 6.3 The farm mainly raises koi carp, but it is also possible to raise other freshwater fish species. They remain in the system for several months before completing their natural growth cycle. Courtesy of the Circle Food and Energy Solutions.

amounts of water, depletes soil quality, and often relies on chemical fertilizers. We wanted to revolutionize this system by integrating aquaponics and vertical farming, creating a closed-loop system where fish waste provides nutrients for plants, and plants purify the water for the fish."

The benefits are immense: we save over 90% of water compared to traditional farming, eliminate the need for chemical fertilizers, and optimize space by growing vertically. However, the challenges are equally significant. Adapting aquaponics for commercial-scale production required extensive research, technical innovation, and overcoming regulatory hurdles. Additionally, educating the market and building trust in new agricultural methods remains an ongoing effort.

They note that aquaponics combines fish farming and hydroponic plant cultivation in a symbiotic system. The process works as follows:

Fish produce organic waste, rich in ammonia.
Biofilters convert ammonia into nitrates, a natural fertilizer for plants.
Plants absorb the nutrients, purifying the water.
Water is recirculated back to the fish, completing the cycle.

This approach drastically reduces water usage, prevents pollution, and enhances food safety by eliminating contaminants like heavy metals and pesticides.

"We have built a strong network of partnerships with universities, research institutions, and private investors. Collaborations with universities such as Rome Tor Vergata and Wageningen University have provided scientific validation and technological advancements. Additionally, support from organizations like the Lazio Region and European Union grants has helped us scale our operations and invest in R&D.

"Anyone interested in the field of aquaponics has to have passion and commitment," according to the founders. "They need vision, especially when facing skepticism. Entrepreneurs must be their first and strongest supporters. While formal education is valuable, gaining practical knowledge in agritech, sustainable systems, and business management is crucial. Securing Capital and Resources—Funding is often overlooked but essential. Look for grants, crowdfunding, and strategic partnerships to support your venture."

As to their future plans:

We aim to expand our aquaponics model globally, particularly in regions struggling with water scarcity and food insecurity. Our research focuses on refining automation, optimizing energy efficiency, and developing new product lines like premium aquaponic-based seasonings. By 2026, we want the Circle to be a global benchmark for sustainable agriculture, proving that high-quality food production and environmental responsibility can go hand in hand.

***

On September 19, 2017, Hurricane Maria, a category five storm with wind speeds of up to 280 kilometers (175 miles) per hour, slammed into Puerto Rico causing total island devastation. The utility power grid and water supply were decimated, and many Puerto Rico's farms were destroyed.

Mayagüez, Puerto Rico: Fusion Farms. "Essentially, we are building an urban farm inside of a hurricane protected building," says Kendell Lang, cofounder and chief executive officer of Fusion Farms.

Fusion Farms is a hurricane-protected vertical aquaponic farm inside a large vacant concrete building in Mayagüez in western Puerto Rico.[6] A hurricane-protected vertical aquaponic farm powered by renewable energy and harvested rainwater. The building protects the farm from tropical storms, harmful pests, temperature extremes, and utility power outages.

The farm uses advanced agriculture techniques and indoor vertical rack systems to grow plants. The farm is capable of growing nine to twelve times the annual yield of traditional farming while using 10 percent less water.

Fusion Farms grows a year-round variety and reliable harvest of fresh food that includes arugula, lettuce, leafy greens, herbs, vegetables, spinach, as well as a range of herbs and spices and fruits. Fusion Farms also markets a fresh sustainable source of fish, such as tilapia.

There are many vacant buildings scattered across the island. Fusion Farms and state government planners are reviewing plans to transform these vacant buildings into hurricane-protected, vertical aquaponic farms.

Fujisawa, Kanagawa, Japan: Aquponi-House. Aquponi is the first company in Japan specializing in aquaponics.[7] Aquponi-House is in Fujisawa, near Tokyo. The company focuses on conducting research and systems related to aquaponics. The company plans to support the building of aquaponic farms in Japan and to sell aquaponics kits for home use.

The company has established the Aquaponics Academy, with both online and in-person courses. The courses offer opportunities for attendees to experiment with working with aquaponic systems in greenhouses. The system includes natural sunlight, as well as indoor systems, using LED lighting. The main produce includes leafy greens such as lettuce and herbs, which have a short harvest cycle and high profitability.

Seaweed Farming

Aquaculture is farming in the water, and seaweed farming is the fastest-growing aquaculture sector. Aquaculture can benefit farmers, communities, and the environment.

Coastline Communities Can Benefit from Seaweed Farms

According to statistics presented at the UN 2017 Ocean Conference, an estimated 2.4 billion people live within ninety-five kilometer (sixty miles) of a coastline. The coastline population represents about 40 percent of the world's population. The people along the coast can benefit from seaweed crops harvested in aquaculture ocean farms and on floating farms. Sea vegetable farms include a large variety of seaweeds and other sea plants. Sea vegetables are excellent nutrient food sources for a growing world population.

> **DID YOU KNOW?**
> Sea vegetable farms about the size of Washington State could provide enough protein for the entire world population, reports Professor Ronald Osinga at Wageningen University in the Netherlands.[8]

Seaweed farming is the fastest-growing aquaculture sector across the world. Seaweed aquaculture benefits farmers, communities, and the environment. The seaweed industry is estimated at $6 billion a year. The industry is expected to increase by more billions in the future when more food will be required for a growing population.

Seaweed aquaculture farms occupy marine environments in oceans and along coastal estuaries. Seaweed aquaculture includes countless species of marine plants and algae that grow in the ocean as well as in rivers, lakes, and other water bodies.

Farmed seaweed is an important source of nutritious food. Seaweed can also be used in a variety of products including medicines, cosmetics, feedstock for animals, and biofuels.

Seaweed farming is sustainable and helps to reduce greenhouse gas emissions by absorbing carbon dioxide from the atmosphere. Seaweed farming involves growing and harvesting different types of seaweed.

Seaweed is a general term used to describe many different species of algae and marine plants. Seaweed can grow in a variety of waters, including the sea, lakes, and rivers. Algae from the sea is generally edible. The seaweed family includes a large variety of seaweed that includes kelp, nori, and dulse.

These seaweeds are an important nutritious food source. The primary mineral components in seaweeds are iodine, calcium, phosphorus, magnesium, iron, sodium, potassium, and chlorine. Native seaweeds contain vitamins C, B_{12}, and E. They contain calcium, protein, and fiber. Seaweeds also contain antioxidants, carotenoids, and flavonoids. Carotenoids have cancer-fighting properties. Flavonoids help prevent cardiovascular disease, diabetes, and cancer.

> **DID YOU KNOW?**
> In the 1960s, Norway pioneered the production of seaweed meal, made from a dried and powdered brown seaweed. It was used as an additive to animal feed.

Edible algae seaweed is classified by color. The most abundant seaweed is brown seaweed, followed by red, green, and blue green seaweeds.

Some of the most popular types of seaweed used in food include the following.

Kombu. Kombu is a Japanese word for a type of kelp. In China it is called Haidari. Kombu (kelp) is a large brown seaweed. and the biggest species. They can measure approximately between two to six meters (six to eighteen feet) long.

Kombu is one of the most popular edible seaweeds in East Asia. These seaweeds can be found in Japan, Russia, China, Tasmanian Islands, Australia, South Africa, the Scandinavian Peninsula, and Canada.

One of the largest producers of kombu is in Hokkaido, the largest island in Japan. Kombu is the main ingredient of dashi, the soup stock in several dishes.

Wakame. Wakame, also known as sea mustard, is a dark green seaweed most often found in miso soup, a traditional Japanese soup. It has a sweet taste, a silky-smooth texture, and is a good source of omega-3 fatty acids. These fatty acids support heart health.

Nori. Most people have seen or eaten nori (Porphym). Nori is a red seaweed used in sushi wrappers. It is the most well-known type of seaweed in the Western world. For at least 1,500 years, the Japanese have wrapped a mixture of raw fish, sticky rice, and other ingredients in a nori.

Dulse. Dulse is a reddish seaweed from the colder waters of the northern Atlantic and northern Pacific oceans. Dulse grows attached to rocks. Dulse was first harvested in Scotland and Iceland more than a thousand years ago.

Dulse has a soft, leathery texture. It has a taste similar to bacon when cooked. It is used in soups, salads, baked into chips, even used as a meat seasoning. The Irish use dulse to make their famous soda bread.

Irish moss. Irish moss is a purple and red alga native to the Atlantic shorelines of the United States and Europe. Irish moss resembles miniature trees. The tiny branches fan out from the stem. Irish moss has a high quantity of carrageenan. Carrageenan is widely used in foods as thickening and gelling agents. Extracts of Irish moss can be found in desserts like tapioca and ice cream.

Sea lettuce. This edible blue-green algae is primarily found along coastlines. Also called green nori, sea lettuce grows in thin, green sheets with wavy, ruffled edges. It looks similar to wilted lettuce. It grows to be fifteen to sixty centimeters (six to twenty-four inches) and usually grows in large masses.

> **DID YOU KNOW?**
> Irish moss got its name during the potato famine in Ireland. People were starving and needed food. They turned to the red algae growing on the rocks.

How Are Seaweeds Farmed?

Seaweeds can be farmed by growing them on long lines. Many of the lines are suspended about one to three meters (four to eight feet) below the surface of the water. Seaweed farming does not require fertilizers, forest clearing, or heavy use of machinery, and, as a result, according to the World Bank, has a negative carbon footprint.

Seaweed farms have been rapidly expanding in China, Indonesia, the Philippines, South Korea, Norway, Canada, and the United States. Seaweed farms alone have the capacity to grow massive amounts of nutrient-rich food.

> **DID YOU KNOW?**
> Some seaweed species, under ideal conditions, can grow up to sixty centimeters (twenty-four inches) in a single day.

United States. U.S. seaweed farming includes dozens of farms in waters in New England, the Pacific Northwest, and Alaska. Maine and Alaska account for more than 80 percent of the U.S. supply of edible seaweed. Farmers grow various types of seaweed. In North America, kelps, which thrive in cold, shallow, nutrient-rich waters, are the most commonly farmed varieties. Other varieties include dulse, bull kelp, and ribbon kelp. They are used to make sushi, salsas, sauces, salads, seasonings, and other food products.

Farmers in Long Island Sound, New York, are exploring small shellfish farms with various species of seaweed. The seaweed will be used to filter out the pollutants and mitigate oxygen depletion. The seaweed will also be used to develop a sustainable source for fertilizer and fish meal.

China. Extensive production of seaweed aquaculture began in China in the 1950s. China is currently the largest producer of edible seaweed. The country produces more than half of the total world's production.

Rongcheng is a city in east China's Shandong Province. It is China's largest seaweed production area. The city is nicknamed the hometown of Chinese seaweed and is known as China's "capital of kelp." In China, kelp is called Haidari. Kelp is the largest species produced, accounting for 67 percent of the national seaweed yield.

South Korea. The Republic of South Korea's dried seaweed exports achieved much success in 2024. Two of the major emerging markets for South Korean seaweed, gim, include the United States and Thailand. Gim is a term for a group of edible seaweeds dried to be used as an ingredient in nutritious food including Korean cuisine.

Philippines. Commercial seaweed farming began in the Philippines in the 1970s. Today seaweed farming is one of the country's most important aquaculture industries. Seaweed farming supports more than 200,000 coastal families.

Commercial seaweed farming in the Philippines was first introduced in the country in the early 1970s; presently the Philippines is the world's fourth largest producer of aquatic plants, including seaweed. The Philippine seaweeds are exported to several countries. They include the United States, China, Spain, Russia, and Belgium. The seaweed provides a carrageenan gelatin-like additive used as a thickening agent and stabilizer for many food and cosmetic products.

Zanzibar, Africa East Coast. Zanzibar is a region of Tanzania, a country on Africa's east coast. Seaweed is a major export crop in Tanzania, Since 1990, Zanzibar has become a primary seaweed producer in Africa. Women farmers harvest seaweed for soap, cosmetics, and medicine. In fact, Zanzibar is famous for its spices. However, ocean pollution, warming waters, and unsustainable farming practices have been a problem for seaweed production.

Japan. Japan has a total of more than 10,000 islands, with a population of over 126 million, extending along the Pacific coast of East Asia. The largest consumers of kelp are the Japanese.

Regenerative Ocean Farming: Seaweeds and Shellfish

Regenerative ocean farming is a method that helps to restore damaged ecosystems by increasing biodiversity, a variety of living things, and removing carbon dioxide from the atmosphere. Seaweed farming is a regenerative practice and can help to reduce greenhouse gas emissions by absorbing carbon dioxide from the atmosphere.

However, besides just seaweed farming, regenerative ocean farming (ROF) can be applied in a variety of ways for growing multiple species in the same area. As an example, ROF can be a model for growing and harvesting both seaweeds and shellfish for food.

The ROF practice of harvesting seaweeds and shellfish requires no freshwater, no feed, and no fertilizers. A sustainable ROF model can benefit coastal communities by increasing food production and food security. The farms can improve water quality and mitigate the effects of ocean acidification in coastal areas.

Shellfish and seaweed aquaculture has emerged as a promising and low-cost tool to help improve water quality. The seaweed, shellfish, and finfish are grown together in a closed-loop system. In the closed-loop system the waste from one species is used as food for another. The seaweed helps clean coastal waters by absorbing carbon dioxide from the water, which protects shelled animals (like oysters) from ocean acidification.

GreenWave: A Regenerative Ocean Farm

"The future of farming is growing oysters, mussels, clams and seaweed on ropes anchored to the ocean floor. So says Bren Smith, a commercial fisherman turned director of GreenWave."

—Time Magazine. The 25 Best Inventions of 2017

GreenWave is a regenerative ocean farm located in coastal waters of Long Island Sound, near New Haven, Connecticut.[9] Bren Smith is co–executive director and cofounder of GreenWave. GreenWave uses a form of agriculture in which more than one species is grown at the same time and space. This underwater vertical farming system grows a mix of seaweeds and shellfish.

The seaweed and mussels grow on floating ropes. The ropes are used to hang baskets filled with scallops and oysters below the surface. The farm grows crops that produce food, fertilizers, animal feed, and more. The catch includes a production of several tons of kelp and a million bivalves, such as mussels and oysters, per hectare per year.

GreenWave has trained and supported thousands of ocean farmers and other interested parties throughout New England, California, New York, the Pacific Northwest, and Alaska. GreenWave provides an ROF Toolkit to provide farmers with tools and a knowledge network to plan, permit, and launch their own farms.

Nemo's Garden, Italy. Nemo's Garden is an underwater farm designed by Sergio Gamberini and team workers.[10] The underwater greenhouse system lies beneath the blue waters off the coast of Noli, Italy, southwest of Genoa. The research project began in 2012.

The underwater greenhouse is composed of several air-filled clear plastic pods, anchored to the bottom of the sea by chains and screws. The pods resemble large balloon-like structures. Each biosphere pod is equipped with sensors for CO_2, O_2, humidity, air temperature, and illumination. The plants inside are grown hydroponically. A nutrient-rich solution delivers water and minerals to the plant roots.

Looking inside the biospheres, you will see water condensing on the inner walls. The dripping condensation keeps the plants watered. The warm, near-constant sea temperature between day and night creates ideal growing conditions. A variety of herbs and crops such as basil, lettuce, and strawberries grow within these pods. An outside water source is only required when initially growing the plants. Cameras are set up to monitor crops continuously. In case of problems, divers can take over.

Floating Farms

Will Cities of the Future Have Floating Farms?

Floating farms refer to agricultural systems located on bodies of water rather than on traditional farmland. The floating farm looks like a mass of floating aquatic plants, mud, and peat. The advantages of using stable floating platforms for food production and raising fish include land-saving, sustainability, and local food access.

Floating farms are in the ocean, on lakes, reservoirs, and even ponds in one's backyard. The platform sizes range from a few meters for small systems to more than 100 meters (300 feet) long for large offshore farms. The platforms are connected in interlocking designs to form rafts. Anchoring is used to maintain proper positioning.

The material commonly used for the building of raised floating platforms include recycled materials from discarded plastic bottles, containers, foam, and timber.

The thickness of the platforms ranges from a few centimeters (inches) to several meters (feet). The platforms can adapt to different water levels and can be moved from one place to another. These floating structures are not vulnerable to flooding, droughts, or soil degradation. Some of the plants that are grown on the floats include watercress, lettuce, kale, spinach, sorrel, Swiss chard, basil, parsley, tomatoes, and strawberries.

Floating farm systems also come with some challenges such as a need to raise the initial funds for the costs for setting up the system. Technical experience is also required to maximize yields and profitability.

The following is a selection of some floating farms.

United States: Cultivating Mussels on Rafts in the Gulf of Maine. The Moretti family farms mussels suspended in rafts floating in the waters off the Casco Bay. Casco Bay is in the Gulf of Maine. Their company, Bangs Island Mussels, began in 1999. The company's mission is to produce nutritious and sustainable seafood that feeds the local communities while regenerating nature and helping the planet.

The Bangs Island Mussels Farm started with three rafts. It now has several more rafts. Each raft is wrapped in protective netting to keep out the ducks.

The farm has harvested thousands of kilograms (pounds) of mussels in a year. Harvesting is done a few times each week.

Rotterdam, Netherlands: The Floating Dairy Farm. Rotterdam is a major European port and second largest city of the Netherlands. The Netherlands is one of the smallest countries in the European Union. The country has more people living below sea level than any other country in the world. The country is also among the world's largest exporters of food products.

Peter van Wingerden is the founder of the Floating Farm in Rotterdam.[11] The three-story floating dairy farm platform houses several cows. The overhead canopies protect the cows from the sun, and they also collect rainwater the cows will eventually drink.

The cows produce raw milk that is later pasteurized for milk and yogurt. The farm supplies dairy products to local consumers.

How does the farm work? The animals are fed on food waste from the city. The food waste includes grain and potato peels from breweries. Other animal food is also collected and supplied by grass clippings from sports fields and golf courses. The cow's waste is collected as manure and is used as a fertilizer for local farms.

Van Wingerden is planning to build two more floating platforms next to the dairy farm. One platform will grow vegetables and the other one will raise chickens.

China. China has a multi-billion-dollar fish farming industry. Fish farming has been a primary source of economy for the country for the past 3,000 years.

The fish farms have been established in the vast waters of the East China Sea, the South China Sea, and the Yellow Sea. China has more than 4.5 million fish farmers, producing nearly two-thirds of the world's cultured seafood, according to the country's Fisheries Bureau. China consumes on average sixty-five million tons of seafood. Most of that seafood, fifty million tons, comes from floating farms. The floating farms cultivate marine crustaceans such as oysters, mollusks, shrimp, and much-sought-after shellfish.

> **DID YOU KNOW?**
> China is considered the birthplace of fish farming.[12]

India. Floating gardens is a concept that is not new to India. The country has floating farm gardens on the Dal Lake in Kashmir.[13] Dal Lake is a freshwater urban lake in the northernmost part of India. Hundreds of houseboats float on the water, including floating gardens.

The floating gardens include special bamboo rafts. The bamboo rafts are built large and heavy to withstand storms. The average size of each raft is about 6 meters, by 2 meters, by .5 meters or (20 ft x 5 ft x 1 ft). The Dal farmers grow vegetables, including cucumbers, tomatoes, spinach, radish, carrots, onion, eggplants, cauliflower, cabbage, and pumpkin in Dal Lake.

The lake's floating farms serve as a major source of vegetable supply to the city of Srinagar, along with fish. The population of Srinagar is more than 1.5 million.

Singapore's Floating Fish Farms. The Republic of Singapore is located in Southeast Asia. The country has a population of approximately 6.2 million residents.

BluCurrent, Singapore. The BluCurrent farm, located off Pasir Ris Coast in the northeast area of Singapore, operates a recirculating aquaculture system (RAS). The system provides an ideal environment for growing fish without hormones or the use of antibiotics.

The offshore farm area includes ten tanks. Each tank can hold up to several tons of fish. The farm uses oxygen-rich water. The system includes raising very young fish, hatchlings right out of their eggs. At the hatchery, the fish are raised to full size. The fish include red snapper and barramundi, an Asian Sea Bass, and other hatchlings. The system recycles water. No waste is released into the ocean. The farm uses solar power to run at least 50 percent of its operations. It can produce up to 350 tons when it operates at full capacity.

Floating Farms in the Philippines. In San Fernando, Philippines, climate is one of the greatest challenges faced by farmers today. The Global Climate Risk Index of 2015 listed the Philippines "as the number one most affected country by climate change."

Between October and mid-November 2024, the Philippines was hit by six consecutive tropical cyclones. Three of the typhoons had wind speeds exceeding 185 km/h (115 mph).

And with each landfall comes the problem of flooding, not just in urban areas, but also in the rural agricultural countryside. A floating farm program is an alternative for both flood-prone and drought-prone areas in the country.[14]

The City of San Fernando is the capital of the province of Pampanga, Philippines. The city has a population of more than 250,000 and many floating farms. The floating farm uses products such as water hyacinths, bamboo, and plastic bottles to construct rafts. The rafts float above the water and are covered with topsoil and organic fertilizer. Several kinds of crops can grow on top of the beds. The crops include vegetables and herbs such as water spinach, legumes, mustard upland tomato, and rice. The vegetables are given to the residents for free, and the floating farms have been able to withstand flooding.

Mexico. Mexico's Floating Gardens are an ancient wonder of sustainable farming. Chinampas were used in Aztec farming. The chinampa is a small human-made island to grow food. Experts say that the chinampas, which have been recognized as a UNESCO World Heritage site, are considered one of the most productive agricultural systems in the world.

7
U.S. URBAN FARMS: CITIES FEEDING THEMSELVES

Cities feeding themselves is an idea that can change the world. An idea whose time has come.
—DR. NICK ROSE, Executive Director,
Sustain: The Australian Food Network

By 2050, approximately 2.5 billion more people will be living in cities, according to a new UN report. This increase is that two out of every three people in the world will be living in cities. In China alone, in the next fifteen years, 350 million Chinese will become urban residents.

How much food will be sufficient to feed the growing population?

The UN Food and Agriculture Organization (FAO) reports that population growth will require farmers to almost double the amount of crops they grow now.[1]

Climate Change Impacts Food Production and Food Insecurity

Growing more food will be a major challenge for many countries. Climate change will impact food production. Droughts, floods, and sea level rise impacts growing crops, raising livestock, and managing fisheries. As an example, by 2050, 2.5 billion urban residents will live in countries where major crop production will decline. These crops include wheat, rice, and corn. Altogether, the wheat, rice, and corn supply at least half the world's dietary energy, according to the FAO.[2]

Reduction of crops leads to food insecurity. Any major reduction of these crops will lead to food insecurity in many cities. During 2023, 13.5 percent (18.0 million) of U.S. households were food insecure at some time, reports the USDA Economic Research Service.[3]

Food insecurity and malnutrition are becoming major urban issues. Lack of access to nutritious food affects the health of millions of children and adults. The UN agencies estimated that more than two billion people do not have regular access to safe, nutritious, and sufficient food.

"Urban farming can improve food security and nutrition, reduce climate change impacts, and lower stress," reports Kotchakorn Voraakhom, an architect who designed Asia's largest urban rooftop farm in Bangkok.[4]

What Is Urban Farming?

Urban farming is not new. The history of urban agriculture dates to about 3,500 B.C., according to the American Society of Landscape Architects (ASLA). Roughly 1,500 years later, aqueducts carried mountain water into the semi-desert towns in Persia for food production.[5] Today, one study estimates that more than 800 million people worldwide practice urban agriculture.

Urban farming is actually what it sounds like—a farm in an urban setting. Urban areas include small-sized and large cities. An average small-sized city would have a population of about 100,000 people. Urban areas also include some land outside the large cities.

Large-city populations can range from hundreds of thousands to several million. Vatican City is the least populated city in the world. It has a population of about 1,000 inhabitants. The city of Tokyo has thirty-seven million people.

Urban agriculture includes the cultivation, processing, and distribution of agricultural products in urban and suburban areas. Presently, you can observe urban farms in backyards, rooftops, on balconies, hanging plants on green walls, in school gardens, childcare centers, aged-care facilities, universities, hospitals, and other similar institutions. Believe it or not, urban farms are also found in abandoned World War II air raid shelters, inside mountain tunnels, caves, and even in the basements of tall buildings.

"Urban agriculture alone will never feed the world. However urban farms can improve natural capital (natural resources) and produce a range of benefits beyond just food." says Dr. Robert Costanza, Professor of Public Policy at the Australian National University and cofounder of the International Society for Ecological Economics.[6]

So, what are the benefits of urban farms besides contributing to food security?

The Range of Benefits of Urban Farming

Green Spaces. Urban farming allows for the creation of green spaces that provide calm and restful spaces. Green spaces include grass, trees, shrubs, and trees.

Air Quality. Plant photosynthesis contributes to the reduction of urban carbon dioxide (CO_2). Green spaces such as rooftop leafy gardens can help reduce levels of air contaminants.

Neighborhood Communication. Urban farming also provides an opportunity for communities to learn about nutrition and the importance of eating a nutritious and balanced diet. There are other benefits, too. Urban farming generates employment, recycles urban wastes, and creates greenbelts. Greenbelts include parks, open spaces, and agricultural lands.

Health and Nutrition. Urban farms can improve food and nutrition by producing and supplying a consistent supply of fresh and healthy food to urban communities and those living in food deserts. Many urban farms also offer hands-on programs and classes to engage local youth by giving them opportunities to gain experience growing food.

The Food Project in Massachusetts hires teenagers to grow hundreds of kilograms (pounds) of food to donate to hunger relief organizations.[7] By working the farm, young people also learn the importance of eating a healthy, balanced diet.

***

Interview

Danielle Andrews, Boston Farms and Greenhouse Manager, The Food Project, Boston, Massachusetts

Andrews is the longtime Boston Farms and Greenhouse Manager at The Food Project. The Food Project is a youth development organization that was founded in 1991, whose work revolves around three core areas, according to Andrews:

- Youth development—Every year, we hire 140 teens from Greater Boston and the North Shore to work on The Food Project's urban and suburban farms. In addition to planting, weeding, and harvesting, these young people participate in educational workshops, lead volunteers, staff farmers' markets, build raised bed gardens, and work with residents of Boston and Lynn to expand food access.

- Food distribution—We grow around 100,000 pounds of food each year on our farms and we operate farmers' markets in Boston and in Lynn. We also donate our produce to a number of nonprofit organizations and food pantries.

Figure 7.1 Danielle Andrews, Boston Farms and Greenhouse Manager of The Food Project. Courtesy of The Food Project.

Figure 7.2 Many plants can grow inside a greenhouse at Boston Farms. Courtesy of The Food Project

- Community empowerment—We build partnerships with community members and organizations to make local, affordable food available to support the health and well-being of all.

Andrews says that prior to arriving at The Food Project, "I worked at a variety of urban and rural sustainable farming operations both in Canada and the United States. My interest in sustainable agriculture was sparked during my undergraduate degree in International Development Studies, where I realized how rapidly policy and politics had impacted how our food is produced. I sought out opportunities to interview local small-scale farmers to learn about the challenges they faced, and this led to a summer internship on a small CSA farm. From there, there was no looking back. I found I liked the long days, the dirty fingernails, the easy connections with strangers over weeding a bed of carrots and the joy of handing over beautiful, healthy produce to appreciative customers. I sought out opportunities on other farms and then pursued a master's degree in environmental education with a focus on sustainable agriculture and education. I grew up in various cities throughout Canada and attended public schools there and then Dalhousie University in Nova Scotia. I am a graduate of the UCSC apprenticeship program in sustainable agriculture and hold a master's in environmental studies from York University in Toronto. I grew up disconnected from farming, but my grandparents were all raised on farms, and my father spent his first few years on the family farm before it was sold. I was raised on stories that captured the challenging beauty of the family farm—the incredibly hard fiscal realities as well as the stories of resilience and the joy of the daily connection to land and the reliance on relationships that are such an important part of farming life."

Andrews emphasized, "I was not a farmer or inclined to outdoor physical work [growing up]! I was in fact known in my family as someone who was always happy to trade away the chore of lawn mowing for bathroom cleaning. I was someone who was social and physically active and loved biking and hiking. Early on in my career I heard Eliot Coleman speak about farming and mentioned that he thought there wasn't another field where people were as supportive of each other as sustainable farming. I've found that to be true. This is a field of hard-working people who know that the tasks we hold are huge, the challenges are many, and we need everyone to be sharing information in order to figure out how to continue to make these small-scale sustainable farms function into the future. I have several farming colleagues that I reach out to for troubleshooting and idea generating—and I love that most of our back to forth happens between 6:00 and 7:00 a.m.! Currently my go-to's are Tim Laird of Powisett Farm in Dover, Massachusetts and Kate of The Neighborhood Farm in Westport, Massachusetts."

Andrews did not expect to pursue work in the sustainable agriculture field. She says, "The reason I took the position on the farm in Nova Scotia that first summer after university was because I wanted to spend a summer in Nova Scotia. I was fortunate to have had a union floor factory job every summer between semesters where I could earn enough money to cover my costs for the school year. I graduated debt-free and with a yearning to spend a summer outside, seeing more of this beautiful province where I had spent four years studying but with little opportunity to see much of the area. I didn't expect to be bitten by the farming bug— but by the end of the summer, all I wanted was to learn more.

"When I was studying at UCSC I spent a few Saturdays volunteering at the Homeless Garden Project in Santa Cruz—that was my first exposure to a project that used agriculture as a social change tool. I thought it was such a special space and I could see how everyone coming into it left changed—from the volunteers to the participants to the CSA members. I had experienced farming as transformational on a personal level, but here I realized that it can be that way for everyone—and I wanted to be part of a movement that connected people to the land, particularly those of us who might not otherwise have the opportunity. This sparked my interest in urban agriculture and what keeps me here. As society becomes increasingly disconnected from nature—I have committed to putting my energy into creating an urban farm that is welcoming of everyone and I see myself as a host and agricultural facilitator—welcoming people of all backgrounds into the task of caring for the earth, and in turn, strengthening our ability to care for each other."

Her advice to looking to enter the field? "When I am hiring for roles associated with our urban farms, I am looking for staff with strong social skills and people with a genuine interest in connecting with others. I need to know that staff like physical work because I know that a big part of our role is supporting others as they relearn the joy of physical labor—something that has been largely lost in recent decades. That said, the amazing thing about agriculture is that anyone who is open to learning can be trained up in the work. I'm less concerned about skill level around agriculture than I am about an openness to others and an understanding of how we all need to contribute to the creation of incredible spaces.

"For folks who want to pursue this work in the long run to take on managing operations of this kind, committing to learning farming is so important and will be time consuming and a lifelong journey. The good news is it is an industry of good-hearted people who love to share knowledge. If you want to combine farming with working in multicultural environments that foster inclusion, this work will also include the ongoing deep personal work that is needed to be an active participant in creating these spaces. There is plenty to be done!"

***

What Do Some of the Future Urban Farms Include?

To the Food and Agriculture Organization of the United Nations, future urban farms will include

- community gardens, soil-based farming, hydroponics;
- parking lots;
- green walls;
- rooftop farms;
- schoolyard gardens; and
- greenhouses.

Presently urban farmers use a variety of technology and skills to grow food. They include regenerative practices and agriculture technology that includes sensors, hydroponics, aeroponics, aquaponics, and vertical farms.

Urban Farming: Regenerative Growing Practices

Urban farmers no longer depend on putting a seed in the ground, watering it, and hoping it will grow. Urban farmers use regenerative growing practices. As mentioned in chapter 3, regenerative agriculture is a system of present and future agricultural practices and principles.

Farmers' practices include no-till or zero tillage. Instead of turning up the soil, they plant cover crops such as clover or certain grasses during off-season times. This is a time when soils might otherwise be left bare. The cover crops protect and build up soil by preventing erosion. Instead of one crop, multiple cropping allows farmers to grow two or more crops, in the same space, during one year. Farmers also use the intercropping method. This method includes growing two or more crops abutting each other in the same field. Composting and mulch applications can improve water conservation by increasing soil organic matter content, which boosts plant health and good soil structure.

Regenerative farming practices support biodiversity, enrich soils, improve watersheds, and increase the capacity of the soil to capture carbon. All of these practices contribute to the reversal of global warming.

Urban Farming: Agriculture Technology (Agritech)

Urban farmers are also implementing AI in agriculture technology to grow food. The list includes drones, robots, sensors, soilless technologies, GPS technology, and vertical farms.

Drones. Drones can be used to deploy beneficial insects or natural predators to control pests in urban farms.

Robots. Urban farm operators can program robots to perform various tasks. The robotic tasks can include monitoring plant growth and health. Robotic carts can be used to plow or fertilize the soil before seed planting takes place. The planting robots provide greater accuracy to the seed sowing process over hands-on efforts. Efficient, dispensing robots are ideal for applying fertilizer and spraying water. These robots can deliver nutrients and administer pesticides.

Sensors. Special tiny, robust sensors are revolutionizing city gardening. Soil sensors include moisture sensors that can adjust irrigation to the ever-changing weather. Temperature sensors ensure the plants are shielded from the extreme weather. Light sensors ensure that each plant receives just the right amount of sunlight.

Soilless Technology. Soilless technologies include hydroponics, aeroponics, and aquaponics. Hydroponics is the process of growing plants in a watery nutrient solution without soil. Aeroponics is another soilless technology for growing plants without soil. In this technology, roots are suspended in the air and irrigated with a nutrient-dense, fog-like mist. Aquaponics is a complete ecosystem that combines aquaculture (fish farming) with hydroponics (fertilizing plants with fish waste nutrients).

Vertical Gardens. The primary goal of vertical farming is to grow and harvest the most crops in a limited space. Farmers can grow vegetables and other crops in high stacked trays inside abandoned warehouses, closed factories, rooftops, greenhouses, and even in shipping freight containers. Farmers can grow plants using indoor and outdoor vertical tower gardens, too.

Urban Farms, United States and Canada

Brooklyn Grange, Brooklyn, New York: Rooftop. Brooklyn Grange is located on the roof of the Brooklyn Naval Dockyard.[8] Brooklyn Grange is a leading rooftop farming and green roofing business. The Grange promotes sustainable urban living by building green spaces and hosting local educational programs and events. The rooftop farms in Brooklyn produce thousands of kilograms (pounds) of organically grown vegetables per year. The rooftop installations help retain much rainfall every time it rains in New York, The installation keeps stormwater out of the city's sewer system and helps to combat overflow problems. Brooklyn Grange's goal is to restore the connection between people and the natural world.

Chicago, Illinois, Windy City Harvest Program: Rooftop. The Chicago Botanic Garden has a soil-based rooftop farm in the Midwest.[9] The farm occupies 1,800 square meters (20,000 square feet). The garden is located on top of McCormick Place. It is the largest convention center in North America. The produce includes kale, collards, carrots, radishes, peppers, beans, beets, cherry tomatoes, and various herbs. These crops were chosen because they are fast growing and well suited to a rooftop setting.

The Windy City Harvest's Youth Farm was first established in 2003 on one acre of land. The youth farm expanded the Chicago Botanic Garden's school and neighborhood gardening education to serve teenagers.

Chicago, Illinois, Growing Home: Organic Farm. "People without jobs are often without roots. They're not tied down, not connected, not part of their family anymore. Our organic farming program is a way for them to connect with nature—to plant and nurture roots over a period of time. When you get involved in taking responsibility for caring for something, creating an environment that produces growth, then it helps you build self-esteem and feel more connected," said Les Brown, founder of Growing Home.[10]

Since 2005, Growing Home has been working in Englewood, a community on Chicago's South Side. Growing Home operates high-production organic farms to train individuals who are eager to work but need a supportive environment to develop their strengths as employees.

Growing Home provides healthy and affordable produce for local communities. In a greenhouse, during each season, you will see a wide variety of vegetables that include beets, brussels sprouts, carrots, celery, leeks, lettuce, onions, parsnips, potatoes, radishes, and spinach. Their farm stands include cooking demonstrations with free samples and recipe cards for healthy meals. Free farm tours are also available.

Chicago, Illinois, City Farm: Organic Farm. City Farm is one of Chicago's oldest urban farms.[11] Vacant fields in urban areas have been turned into organic farms using compost collected through the City Farm collective. The urban farm grows a variety of crops annually including tomatoes, kale, collards, beets, herbs, salad greens, cucumbers, rainbow chard, Malabar spinach, garlic, and more. The farm sells to the local community and local restaurants with a percentage of crops going directly to food banks and pantries in the immediate community.

> **DID YOU KNOW?**
> What is the highest rooftop farm in the world? The Bank of America Tower is in Hong Kong. The rooftop container farm is thirty-nine stories above ground.

Alemany Farm, San Francisco, California: Organic Farm. Alemany Farm is a 1.4 hectare (3.5 acre) organic farm located in southeast San Francisco. It is the largest urban farm in San Francisco. The farm's mission is to increase local food security. All of the produce grown at the farm is given away for free. The farm has produced and donated tons of fruit and vegetables since 2009.

The rows on the land enable farmers to grow forty-five different varieties of vegetables throughout the year. The farm also has an "urban orchard" nearby. The orchard has many fruit trees growing different types of fruit. The fruit trees grow everything from apples and pears to plums and pineapple guavas.

Oakland, California, Acta Non Verba: Youth Urban Farm Project. Acta Non Verba (ANV) is a youth urban farm program.[12] It is located behind a recreation center in Oakland, California. The community is a USDA-defined "food desert," with only a few grocery stores within five kilometers (three miles) providing limited fresh produce.

Kelly Carlisle is the founder and executive director of Acta Non Verba. She is a navy veteran and a master gardener. ANV creates a safe and creative outdoor space for children, youth, and families. The goal of ANV is to engage and strengthen young people's understanding of nutrition, food production, healthy living, and their ties to the community.

The food is planned, harvested, and sold by local elementary and middle school–aged students. The food includes peppers, strawberries, squash, and five varieties of tomatoes. The farm includes cooking classes, community building events, and educational childcare camps.

Kelly Carlisle received the 2019 Renewal Summit Award at a ceremony in New York City. The awards highlighted the policy makers, community leaders, entrepreneurs, artists, and urbanists making a difference in their cities around the country.

Hamilton, Ohio, 80 Acres Farms: Vertical Farm. Based in Hamilton, Ohio, 80 Acres Farms is a vertical farming operation. It has eight locations in four states. All of the farms use zero pesticides and less water consumption compared to traditional farms. The farms grow a range of salad blends, microgreens, and herbs plus a grab-and-go salad and protein kit, baby cucumbers, and cherry tomatoes. 80 Acres is capable of robotically planting, harvesting, and packaging hundreds of tons of leafy greens annually.

Atlanta, Georgia: Metro Atlanta Urban Farm. The Metro Atlanta Urban Farm's goal is to reduce barriers to healthy living in urban communities. This program offers assistance to more than one hundred new and existing gardens across Metro Atlanta. Volunteers and neighbors come together to grow fresh, healthy food to nourish communities and neighborhoods. The farms grow several varieties of tomato as well as okra, canola greens, kohlrabi, Swiss chard, spinach, various varieties of lettuce, turnips, and collards.

Cleveland, Ohio: Ohio City Farm. Located in Cleveland, Ohio, the Ohio City Farm is one of the largest urban farms in the United States. With more than 2.4 hectares (5 acres), the farm aims to provide fresh, local, and healthy food to Cleveland's underserved residents. The farmers grow and sell organically farmed fresh produce to urban residents and city workers. The fresh produce includes beets, garlic, peppers, leafy greens, and tomatoes.

Ohio City Farm is operated by Re:Source Cleveland (formerly The Refugee Response) a nonprofit that works to empower immigrant newcomers such as refugees to become self-sufficient and contributing members of their new communities.

Seattle, Washington: Rainier Beach & Wetlands Urban Farm. Rainier Beach Urban Farm & Wetlands is a city park where people come together to grow food and work to restore the wetlands through powerful partnerships.[13] The farm is a four-hectare (ten-acre) site dedicated to organic food production and distribution, environmental education, and wetland restoration. The farm grows an abundance of fresh vegetables, herbs, fruit, flowers, eggs, honey, and other agricultural products. The farm offers live, online classes on topics such as veggie gardening, container gardening, canning and pickling, beekeeping, raising chickens, and more.

Baltimore, Maryland: Real Food Farm. Real Food Farm is an urban farm in northeast Baltimore's Clifton Park. This site is home to hoop garden houses, outdoor growing fields, and beehives. The Real Food Farm occupies Clifton Park and Perlman Place.

Clifton Park covers about 2.5 hectares (6 acres) of land in the park. This site is home to hoop houses, outdoor growing fields, a sensory garden, and more than 100 fruit trees. As a resource for other urban farms, this site has a large gas-heated greenhouse and a solar-powered walk-in refrigerator that is used by the farm and others.

Perlman Place installed perennial beds to help reduce the farm's stormwater runoff. The flowering plants attract pollinators, and they beautify the farm. The farm's orchard contains fig trees, Asian pears, and Asian persimmons.

Jackson, Mississippi: Foot Print Farms. "We Have to Serve Those Most in Need." Dr. Cindy Ayers Elliott is CEO and founder of Foot Print Farms, the state's largest urban growing operation.[14] Foot Print Farms is a twenty-seven-hectare (sixty-eight-acre) farm that grows fruits and vegetables and raises goats and cattle.

Established in 2010, Foot Print Farms continues to impact the community with their work. The farm trains and teaches young farmers how they can grow some of their own food. The Foot Print farmers deliver locally farm fresh produce to many Jackson neighborhoods where many people live in food deserts that lack stores that sell healthy and affordable food. Cindy Ayers Elliott was *USA TODAY*'s Women of the Year 2023 honoree for Mississippi.

Austin, Texas: Urban American Farmer. Urban American Farmer is an organization based in Austin, Texas.[15] Trisha Bates, Founder + Farmer of Urban American Farmer, focuses on building networks between city and country, farmer and chef, human and land. Trisha Bates offers a variety of services focused on food education to help transform urban space into food production sites.

The organization is working to build a communication network that engages both farmers and chefs. The organization provides a Kitchen Garden Workshop Program. During the twelve-week workshop, participants learn how to grow their own kitchen gardens at home or at their restaurant.

In 2021, Bates launched the first season of Farm School for Chefs on an urban farm less than a mile from downtown Austin. Presently Urban American Farmer hosts farming courses to increase consumer awareness about sustainable food sourcing and growing practices. Ten restaurant teams grew their own food in hundred-foot rows right next to each other. Farmers attended weekly class sessions about soil, seasonality, pest management, and much more. The food they grew, from seed to harvest, is used in their restaurants for dishes or family meals. In total, the program hosted three seasons of farm school, reaching hundreds of culinary professionals.

Oakland, California, Planting Justice: Urban Farm. Gavin Raders and Haleh Zandi are the founders of Planting Justice in East Oakland, California.[16]

Presently, eighty-five formerly imprisoned people have full-time jobs at Planting Justice. The program unveils that people who are incarcerated can successfully come home, heal, and stay with their families and communities.

The farm includes three urban garden/nurseries and two farms. Some of the vegetables grown, all season, include cucumbers, zucchini, squash, okra, peppers, pole beans, tomatoes, and watermelon. Food from the farm is distributed free to schools.

Seattle, Washington: The P-Patch Community Gardening Program. The P-Patch Community Gardening Program is managed by Seattle Department of Neighborhoods. The program is made up of open spaces in Seattle neighborhoods. The gardens are built on public property owned by various city departments and by public and private owners. Gardeners use small plots of land to grow organic food, flowers, and herbs.

As of December 2023, there are ninety P-Patch community gardens, and more than 3,750 gardeners. Several of the gardens have programs, designated as "giving garden" plots in which the food is grown for food banks and hot meal programs. In 2023, the gardeners donated more than 15,000 kilograms (33,438 pounds) of produce.[17]

Washington, DC: Common Good City Farm. Common Good City Farm's mission is to sustain and support a community through growing, learning, cooking, and sharing fresh food together. The Common Good City Farm grows about 6,000 pounds of food each year to share with their community. In 2023, the farm grew about 3,000 kilograms (6,517 pounds) of organic produce across their five farm sites! The farm grows spring, summer, and fall crops that include everything from carrots, cabbage, lettuces, radishes, cucumbers, eggplants, kale, apples, and herbs and flowers. The farm sites include a fruit orchard, beehives, and compost system.

Since January 2007, Common Good has provided fresh produce to the community and has engaged more than 2,700 adults and 4,500 young people in educational programs. Common Good City Farm's programs provide hands-on training in food production, healthy eating, and environmental sustainability. Throughout the year, they offer Seed to Table workshops about gardening, nutrition, and cooking. On the education front, the workshops served many students through their Little Sprouts garden program. The farm provides more than $30,000 in direct support to local urban farmers, food producers, and community gardeners.[18]

U.S. Department of Agriculture (USDA)

Urban Farming and Innovative Production

In conclusion, the Department of Agriculture (USDA) assists urban, small-scale, and other producers with procedures for growing and managing crops and selling advice. The agency provides technical and financial assistance for a variety of farm work and operations. They include community farms and gardens, rooftop, indoor, and vertical farms, and hydroponic, aeroponic, and aquaponic facilities. Grants are also available to initiate or increase efforts of farmers, gardeners, citizens, schools, cities, tribes, and other stakeholders. The grants are funded to expand food production, provide training and education, support infrastructure needs, encourage climate-resilient practices, and more. In 2022, the USDA invested $14.2 million in fifty-two grants that support urban agriculture and innovative production.

8
GLOBAL URBAN FARMS: CITIES FEEDING THEMSELVES

Urban Farms North of the Border

Canada

Our neighbors to the north have their own system of urban agriculture, and it's deeply rooted in Canadian culture. The first settlers in French Canada grew "potagers" or kitchen gardens, which turned into victory gardens during WWII.

Saskatchewan, Canada. Saskatchewan is a province in western Canada. It has a special project that offers youth internships to encourage both indigenous groups such as the Cree community and nonindigenous students to learn about and participate in urban agriculture. The Cree are a North American indigenous people. They live primarily in Canada, where they form one of the country's largest First Nations. More than 350,000 Canadians are Cree or have Cree ancestry.

The urban agriculture project, called kiscikânis, means garden in Cree.[1] The site grows vegetables, flowers, and herbs in containers in the heart of Saskatoon's west side (Saskatoon is the largest city in Saskatchewan). Project participants use container gardens to grow plants in modified barrels. With well over a hundred containers in use, the container garden is an excellent way to get young people involved.

About 1,400 kilometers (860 miles) from the province of Saskatchewan is British Columbia and the city of Vancouver, a city with urban farms.

Vancouver's Urban Farms. The city of Vancouver is in the southwest corner of the province of British Columbia. It is surrounded on three sides by water. The city is divided into several neighborhoods with a population of more than two million people. For more than fifteen years, Sole Food Street Farm has been an urban agriculture project in Vancouver.[2] Sole Food's mission is to provide low-income residents with agricultural training and jobs.

Sole Food currently operates farms in four locations. Crops are planted in specially designed boxes. The boxes keep the crops separate from the soil or concrete below. In addition, all boxes are built on shipping pallets. This practice allows the plants to be moved with a forklift on short notice if needed. In July 2013, Sole Food opened an urban orchard and planted 500 trees at the orchard. In the orchard, several types of fruits, such as apple and pear, and different types of herbs are grown.

Urban Farms South of the Border

Mexico City, Mexico: Rooftops. Mexico City is one of the largest urban centers in the world. The city has an estimated population of twenty-two million. Mexico City residents often grow food using rooftop gardens. The municipal government has issued grants to more than 3000 city residents since 2007. As a result of these grants, there has been an increase in people using rooftop cultivation.

The borough of Milpa Alta is on the outskirts of the capital city. About 20 percent of the working population engages in a variety of growing food. Many have home gardens. One of the primary crops of Milpa Alta is Nopal cactus. Nopal is referred to as a "prickly pear cactus" in English. The paddles of the plant (no spines) are high in soluble fiber, vitamin C and other vitamins, and minerals.[3]

Mexico is a large country, home to more than 130 million people. Researchers are now studying the effects of vertical farming as new companies attempt to introduce the concept in Mexico. Vertical farming has gained traction in recent years because it gives people the opportunity to grow food in cities and areas where the population is rapidly increasing. Estimates indicate that Mexico's population could rise to 150 million citizens by 2050; therefore, it is important to ensure that food production increases over the next several decades.

Medellín, Columbia. The city's population is more than two million. The mayor's office has a program called Huertas con Vos (Urban and Rural Kitchen Gardens with You). The program is designed to ensure that these small family gardens will grow, thrive, and multiply. The Medellín government developed this program to ensure food security and healthy eating for the residents in their city.[4]

Anyone with at least ten square meters (approximately 100 square feet) to spare can take part in the program. Gardeners are given the tools and seeds they need to get started. Gardeners also have access to workshops that teach how to plant and care for their gardens.

São Paulo, Brazil: Organic Farms. São Paulo area is home to more than twenty million people. The Cidades Sem Fome (Cities without Hunger) was founded in 2004 in São Paulo by Hans Dieter Temp.[5] Temp is a technician for agriculture and environmental policies.

Cities without Hunger is establishing community organic gardens in the favelas in the East Zone of São Paulo. Favela is a Portuguese term for several types of impoverished neighborhoods in Brazil. Favelas are found in urban areas throughout Brazil.

Cities without Hunger develops community gardens, school gardens, and greenhouses on public and private unused land. The gardeners sell their fresh vegetables to the residents in the favelas at affordable prices. The São Paulo urban farmers are constantly on the lookout for underused spaces to produce local food and to help the local economy.

Caracas, Venezuela. Caracas is the capital of Venezuela with a population of three million inhabitants. The Bolívar 1 Organoponic Garden is a two-acre plot in the center of Caracas.[6] Organoponic is a system of urban agriculture using organic gardens. The Bolívar 1 project is affiliated with the Urban Agriculture Ministry. Bolívar 1 has distinct zones in the city such as the "White Zone" for leafy greens and the "Orange Zone" for other crops such as peppers, leeks, and spring onions. There are 150 plant beds in total. Along one side is a traditional garden with perennial crops such as mango, soursop, avocado, and plantain.

The farm production is free from agrochemicals. Farmers use no industrial fertilizers or chemical pesticides. Instead, farmers make their own fertilizers and use a variety of plants to keep pests away. Some of the plans include color traps such as sunflowers and medicinal plants that repel harmful insects. Farmers also use nutrients that come from livestock to fertilize the garden. They employ horse manure to balance soil acidity. The famers can draw potassium, calcium, and iron from certain seeds to nourish the ground and increase yields. Wind barriers are created with sugarcane.

Urban Farms in Europe

Urban farming in Europe is not new. In fact, several countries encouraged the production of food in urban environments during both the First and Second World Wars in the twentieth century. Today, startup urban agriculture enterprises are cropping up across the continent. And guess which European country has the largest urban farm in the world?

Agripolis Farms, Paris, France. Rooftop. The largest urban farm in the world opened in 2020 in Paris, France.[7] The new farm is at the top of a six-story building in the heart of the French capital. The farm is about 14,000 square meters (150,000 square feet). The top of the building is home to twenty farms growing thirty different crops. The Marais district, in Paris, has produced 900 kilograms (2,000 pounds) of vegetables and fruits per day.

Urban agriculture is now flourishing in France. The city of Paris created the Parisculteurs project that promotes that one third of the land is to be dedicated to urban agriculture. Since 2021, the city of Paris has committed to planting 100 hectares (247 acres) of vegetation across the capital.

Mudchute Park and Farm, London, England. The Mudchute Park and Farm, in East London, is one of the largest city farms in Europe.[8] The size of the farm and park is 13 hectares (32 acres). Mudchute Park and Farm is home to more than 100 animals that include rabbits, chickens, goats, pigs, sheep, and even llamas. The farm grows vegetables, but it is also a park where children can pet the animals. A few of the major objectives for the farm and park is to give local people the opportunity of recreation and leisure on the Mudchute and to provide education and training for young people.

Spitalfields City Farm, London, England. Spitalfields City Farm is the nearest city farm to London. Education is one of the core parts of the farm's purpose and mission. Its goal is to bring animal and horticulture experiences to thousands of children every year.

Visitors can see several outdoor green spaces where staff and volunteers grow vegetables and raise farm animals. The farm includes both polytunnels and greenhouses to grow plants. Polytunnels are made from steel and covered in plastic. The greenhouses are made from glass with metal frames. These structures provide a yearlong warm climate to grow plants and protect them from extreme cold.

The farm grows a wide range of seasonal flowers, radishes, beans, basil and other herbs, fruit, and vegetables. Wildflowers and herbs are grown among the vegetables. The garden includes a shelter with a seating area built with cedar trunks and recycled scaffold planks. Large troughs are used to catch rainwater from the shelter's roof.

The farmyard is home to a variety of animals such as donkeys, pigs, goats, cows, sheep, and chickens. Staff and volunteers take part in the animals' daily care. The volunteers get the opportunity to learn about animal care and needs.

Berlin, Germany. The capital city of Germany was once divided by the Berlin Wall. The city of Berlin now includes urban farming. Many of the projects are very mobile. Therefore, these gardens can be moved to accommodate changes in land ownership.

One of the urban gardens is located on the grounds of the Berlin Tempelhof Airport. The Berlin Airlift of 1948–1949 made the airport a symbol of freedom. Now the soil of the landing field is used by local residents to grow fruit and vegetables.

Andernach, Germany: The Edible City. Andernach is a city about 621 kilometers (385 Miles) south of Berlin. Andernach, with a population of around

30,000 people, is known as an "edible city." It means that many of the public green spaces are used to grow food.[9]

By making edible plants a feature of public space, the town has changed the way locals think about their food. The public vegetable beds are accessible to everyone and can also be harvested by all citizens. The city center has fruit and vegetable gardens that anyone can harvest for free. The Edible City program centers on long-term and sustainable management of green spaces. The green spaces enable the city to promote socializing among its citizens.

Barcelona, Spain: Small Plot Gardens. In Barcelona, the Department of the Environment provides a network of urban gardens that includes a citizen participation program.[10] The program is addressed to citizens over sixty-five years old. The objective is aimed at attracting local seniors into environmental improvement activities. One of the activities is learning how to grow vegetables by following the principles of organic farming. The seniors grow the plants in small plots. Each plot is between 23 square meters (250 square feet) to 37 square meters (400 square feet) in which vegetables and herbs and seasonal flowers are grown.

Bologna, Italy: Community Garden of Via Gandusio. There are an estimated eighteen million urban gardens currently in Italy. The following is one of the urban gardens.[11] Via Gandusio is a housing complex in the north of Bologna. At the Via Gandusio, there is a large rooftop garden. In 2011, it became the first rooftop garden of Bologna and of Italy.

Via Gandusio is occupied by two different communities. They include elderly Italians and international immigrants from Africa and Asia. To bring the communities closer together socially, a community garden was designed by the Municipality of Bologna.

The goal was to provide a meeting place for everyone in the Via Gandusio to get together. The mixed community plans a garden and grows a variety of vegetables. The vegetables include lettuce, chicory, tomatoes, peppers, melons, watermelon, eggplant, and herbs. All of the plants are grown using a hydroponics system for growing plants.

Urban Farms in Asia

Several Asian countries have invested significant amounts in urban farming technologies as a way of dealing with population growth and combating food insecurity.

Seoul, South Korea. Seoul is aiming for more urban farming with financial and professional support offered by local government offices. These government grants are meant to supply 80–100 percent of the funding needed to get urban farms up and running. Urban agriculture has grown six-fold over a seven-year period.[12]

One of the developments in Seoul's urban farming community comes in the form of smart vertical farms, including Metro Farm, a hydroponic farm placed in a subway station. The operation has proven so popular and successful that its developers have now installed four more in other stations throughout the urban center.

Pakistan. Pakistan's first vertical farm was developed in the Sindh Industrial Trading Estate in Karachi. The population of Karachi is more than twenty million; it is the third-largest city in the world. The owner had a background in environmentally friendly and futuristic plant growth technologies and wanted to convert them into a business model.[13] The vertical farm, located in a previous yarn factory, has been actively producing fresh vegetables and supplying them to multiple restaurants and clients around the city. Almost 2,500 plants of kale, cherry tomatoes, pak choi, iceberg lettuce, Swiss chard, wild rocket, Thai basil, green and colored capsicum, jalapenos, micro greens, parsley, celery, oregano, rosemary, thyme, and sage are grown within a cycle of forty-five to sixty days from the time of seeding to harvesting.

Indonesia. In 2017, the city of Jakarta initiated a peri-urban farming program under its Urban Agriculture Program. As of 2024, more than 500 community farms were established in the city. The urban farms consisted in using vacant lots and private yard lands for growing vegetables, fruits, spices, and even some medicines. One of the communities included sustainable organic urban farming. The farm products supported more than 3500 residents.[14]

India. Urban farming in India has emerged, and grown significantly. India is facing the challenges posed by rapid urbanization. Urban farming also offers employment for many households. Residents of India's urban areas are cultivating crops on rooftops, balconies, and vacant lots, which is quietly leading to an urban farming movement.

Bihar. Bihar is situated in the eastern part of India. Bihar is home to nearly one hundred million people. The government is working toward urban farming on a large scale. The plan is for the state government to pay half the funds needed to start a rooftop farm. These farms would then provide healthy food and much-needed greenery for the city. Urban citizens would be given training in rooftop growing and the supplies they need, and gain extra income from selling their crop.[15]

Bengaluru: Urban Farming in Bengaluru. Bengaluru, also known as Bangalore, is the capital and largest city of the southern Indian state of Karnataka. The state is in southwestern region of India. The population of the capital is more than thirteen million. Rooftop gardens are becoming increasingly popular in Bangalore, providing various environmental and social benefits. The rooftop gardens help reduce the urban heat island effect, provide natural insulation that reduce energy consumption, and improve air quality. Residents and businesses are transforming their rooftops into green spaces, combating pollution and promoting biodiversity. Their innovative rooftop gardens provide better access to more nutritious food.

Vertical farming is also found in Bangalore's urban spaces. The vertical farming practices involve growing crops in vertically stacked layer. By bringing food production closer to urban centers, vertical farms help reduce carbon emissions and offer several benefits over conventional farming practices, such as higher crop yields, reduced water usage, and year-round production.

Delhi: Urban Farms in Delhi. Urban farming is flourishing in Delhi. From rooftop gardens and vertical farming setups to community plots and innovative hydroponic systems, residents and organizations are cultivating green spaces to promote local food production, reduce environmental impact, and foster healthier urban lifestyles.

Delhi's urban farming movement is characterized by the creative use of underutilized spaces. Rooftops, balconies, vacant lots, and even walls have been transformed into thriving green oases. Rooftop farming, in particular, has gained significant traction across the city. These gardens not only provide fresh, organic produce but also help in combating the heat island effect, reducing the overall temperature of urban areas. Delhi has embraced the innovative technique of aquaponics, which allows for the harmonious cultivation of both verdant vegetables and vibrant fish within a self-sustaining, closed-loop system.

Mumbai: Vertical Farming. Mumbai is the sixth-most-populous metropolitan area in the world with a population of over twenty-three million. Kisano is a vertical farming company based in Mumbai. Founded in 2018, the Kisano vertical farm grows and provides fruits and vegetables without the need for pesticides, herbicides, or other chemicals.

Singapore. Singapore is a city-state and country in Southeast Asia. Singapore is the largest port in Southeast Asia and one of the busiest in the world. Nearly two-thirds of the main island is less than fifteen meters (fifty feet) above sea level. Little of the land area is classified as agricultural, and production contributes a negligible amount to the overall economy. Urban farming is important in Singapore because the country depends heavily on imported foods. The city-state imports 90 percent of its food. As a result, Singapore is a country with the most urban farming.

By 2030, the Singapore Food Agency's (SFA's) goal for the country is to produce 30 percent of its own nutritional needs.

Edible Garden City. The Edible Garden City (EGC), a former compound in the largest prison in Singapore, is now an urban farm.[16] The mission of Edible Garden City is to inspire, engage, and make it possible for people to grow their own food in Singapore.

The Edible Garden City was cofounded by local resident Bjorn Low in 2012. EGC is one of Singapore's urban farming efforts to strengthen the island's food security. "Our goal was and is to encourage more locals to grow their own food and thus help strengthen the city's food resilience," says Sarah Rodriguez, EGC's head of marketing.

Presently there are more than 250 gardens. The gardens include vegetables and herbs. Currently, EGC grows kale and chard using hydroponics and grows microgreens in soil. All of the farming is in a climate-controlled, indoor environment. The produce is distributed among restaurants, hotels, schools, and homes in Singapore.

Aquaponics in Singapore: Fairmont Singapore and Swissotel. The guests at the Fairmont Singapore and Swissotel enjoy food prepared from the hotels' rooftop aquaponics farm. The farm includes fish tanks, tower gardens, and LED lights above the plants. The aquaponics farm is 450 square meters (4,800 square feet) and is capable of producing more than 1,200 kilograms (2,600 pounds) of vegetables and 350 kilograms (660 pounds) of fish monthly.

As of June 2024, the population of Singapore is 6.04 million. Since the city-state currently only produces less than 10 percent of food requirements locally, the Singaporean government has actively backed starters of urban farms in the city state with grants.

Manila, Philippines. Urban farming is becoming a popular trend in the Philippines. More and more people are recognizing the benefits of growing food in the city. Future Fresh in Manila provided a head start on indoor farming in the Philippines.[17] Future Fresh is an aeroponic vertical farm that grows specialty greens all year long. The produce includes lettuce, basil, spinach, parsley, arugula, herbs, and kale.

The indoor vertical farms use a minimal amount of water and no pesticides or agrochemicals in their growing process. By being indoors, the farm is unaffected by climate change or weather conditions. At Future Fresh, they produce and deliver all of their produce directly to the customers.

Dhaha, Bangladesh: Rooftop Gardens. The City of Dhaka is in Bangladesh in South Asia. The city's population exceeds fifteen million residents. Air pollution is a major concern. Rooftop gardens, with a variety of plants, are helping to solve the pollution problem. The rooftop garden includes a variety of fruits and vegetables. The plants have the potential to reduce pollutants in the air and improve air quality. As a result, the air is getting cleaner and fresher in the densely populated city.

China

China is investing significant amounts of effort into developing vertical farming systems to feed its urban population. By 2050, 80 percent of the population will live in cities. China's population is projected to reach 1.5 billion in 2030, and agricultural land is diminishing. Meanwhile the demand for food is increasing.

China has become a major leader in indoor vertical farming. "Vertical farming is going to become important everywhere, and China does have these massive populations inside cities because people are leaving the countryside into the cities," said Roger Royse, a lawyer and founder of AgTech Innovation Network in Silicon Valley.[18]

Shanghai. Shanghai is a city in east central China, with a population of more that twenty-four million. The city has preserved and expanded a green agricultural zone. Shanghai now produces more than 55 percent of its vegetables and 90 percent of its green-leaf vegetables. The nutrients from waste are recycled to help produce more than half the city's vegetables. Shanghai is one of the most densely populated cities in the world, with all of the accompanying pollution and congestion. To clear the air and feed its growing population, the city is embracing urban farming. Laogang is an enormous trash dump of about 6.5 square kilometers. It now composts about 80 percent of the organic material that enters its gates, turning it into potent fertilizer. This fertilizer is then used in the city's agricultural zone, where the municipal government produces about 55 percent of the vegetables.

One of the Shanghai organic farms is made from recycled shipping containers. Inside, the plants grow with a water filtration and circulation system. The systems provide water resource management and protection from pollutants.[19]

Beijing. Beijing is in north China and has devoted considerable resources to applying new technologies to the urban agriculture sector. The population is more than twenty million residents. The goal is to maximize efficiency and rationally utilize scarce water and land. Different types of rainfall harvest technologies are being piloted in the downtown area for watering parks and rooftop plantations. Drip irrigation systems have been introduced for most greenhouses and farms within the city. To combat air pollution, a new forest has been started on the outskirts of the city, with a planned area of over 6,000 hectares (14,800 acres).

Japan

Tokyo: Pasona Urban Rooftop Farm. In Japan, more than a thousand small farms continue to grow crops. "Urban agriculture not only provides citizens with fresh, safe, and reliable agricultural products," says Ryoto Matsuzawa, of the Agriculture Affairs Committee of the Tokyo Metropolitan, "it also preserves the environment and offers disaster preparedness."

Pasona is a Japanese recruitment company. The Pasona Headquarters is located in a downtown Tokyo building.[20] The Pasona Urban Farm is in the building, nine stories high, with a rooftop garden. The rooftop garden allows employees to grow and harvest their own food at work. The garden includes hundreds of species of plants that include fruits, vegetables, and rice. The plants are harvested, prepared in a kitchen, and served in the indoor cafeterias in the building.

The rooftop is not the only place to see plants growing. Walking in the hallways, you can observe plants growing inside and outside the offices. In one place, tomato vines are suspended above conference tables. Lemon and passion fruit trees are used as partitions for staff meetings. To keep the indoors healthy for plants and people, a control system is used. The control system monitors humidity, temperature, and airflow inside the building.

Pasona focuses on educating the next generation of farmers. The company offers public seminars, lectures, and internship programs. The programs provide students with case studies, management skills, and financial advice. The program's goal is to promote both traditional and urban farming as a profession and as a business opportunity.

Egypt

Cairo, Egypt. Cairo is the capital of Egypt and the country's largest city, with a population of ten million. The country is located in northeast Africa.

Cairo has an urban farm called Schaduf. The Arabic word "schaduf" refers to an ancient irrigation tool. The tool was used to lift water from a well to irrigate land. Schaduf has transformed Cairo's rooftops into hydroponic farms to grow local, organic sources of fresh vegetables. The vegetables include lettuce, parsley, dill, coriander, spinach, and more. The farms help low-income residents grow their own vegetables. Schaduf provides technical training for many farmers at centers located throughout Cairo's neighborhoods.

Urban Farms in Sub-Saharan Africa

Sub-Saharan Africa is a sub-continent located in Africa. Sub-Saharan Africa includes countries in central Africa, east Africa, southern Africa, and west Africa. The estimated population of sub-Saharan Africa is 1,273,663,761.

GLOBAL URBAN FARMS

Many of these countries have urban farms. The following is a selection of urban farms in some of the countries.

Nairobi, Kenya. By 2050, over half of Kenyans will live in urban areas. Urban farming provides a localized approach to food production, reducing dependence on distant rural sources and offering a means to secure supplies. Vertical gardens, rooftop farms, community gardens, and hydroponics maximize space, enabling cultivation of a wide variety of crops, including tomatoes, potatoes, lettuces, carrots, herbs, and even edible flowers. For instance, some urban farms repurpose old empty parking structures to grow mushrooms. Tomatoes and peppers are two of the most popular fruit-bearing vegetables for urban farms.

Accra, Ghana. Ghana is a country in west Africa. It is on the coast of the Gulf of Guinea. The population is more than thirty-three million people. Accra is the capital of Ghana and the largest city with a population of nearly three million. The main staple food crops are maize, yams, cassava, rice, taro (cocoyam), plantain, and other root crops. The fruit crops include pineapples, bananas, mangoes, papayas, and citrus.

Urban farming in Ghana has every type of agricultural production within the city. They include everything from small family gardens to larger operations raising export crops. They include household or home gardening, and open or vacant-space cultivation. The Food and Agriculture Organization (FAO) is driving sustainable development in Ghana through its Country Programming Framework (CPF), promoting climate resilience.

Ethiopia. One of Africa's biggest cities, Addis Ababa, is Ethiopia's capital. In 2025, population was estimated at 5,956,680.[21]

Farm Africa works across Ethiopia, helping people who rely on the land to improve their livelihoods and restore their ecosystems. The charity promotes sustainable agricultural practices, strengthens markets, and protects the environment in rural Africa.

Farm Africa is a UK-based charitable organization set up in 1985. The mission is to work with farmers, pastoralists, and forest communities in eastern Africa. Farm Africa has been supporting low-income urban communities to grow their own produce. Participants have grown a range of crops including cabbages, carrots, beetroot, and lettuce, and have reared chickens and fish. The year-round availability of leafy green vegetables and poultry products has also had a positive impact on nutrition and food security. However, disruptions in rainfall patterns, more frequent and severe droughts, and soil degradation can reduce crop productions in many countries, including Ethiopia.

9
AGRICULTURAL LITERACY, CLIMATE LITERACY, AND EDUCATION

Agriculture is everything involved with growing plants and animals to be used for something else. Nearly everything we eat, wear, and use comes from a plant or an animal raised on a farm.
—CINDY HALL, Education Program Manager,
Iowa Agriculture Literacy Foundation[1]

The Role of Modern Agriculture

"Agriculture is one of the world's largest industries. It employs more than one billion people and generates over $1.3 trillion dollars' worth of food annually. Pasture and cropland occupy around 50 percent of Earth's habitable land and provide habitat and food for a multitude of species. Food drives the world; apart from clean water, access to adequate food is the primary concern for most people on Earth. Agricultural productivity is important not only for a country's balance of trade but the security and health of its population as well."[2] The Bureau of Economic Analysis reports that agriculture, food, and related industries contributed about $1.537 trillion to U.S. gross domestic product (GDP) in 2023. The sector accounts for about 10 percent of total U.S. employment, more than twenty-two million jobs.[3]

What Do We Know about Agriculture?

How often do adults and young people think about agriculture? Where does our food come from? Who grows it? How does it get to our table?

As mentioned previously, "Most adults and young people know very little about agriculture and its value in their daily lives. Agriculture illiteracy is one of the top twenty illiteracies in our country today. Many people are never informed of the importance that agriculture has and agriculture is entirely too important to be ignored," says Brittany Taylor, Future Farmers of America (FFA).[4]

Agriculture plays a vital role in virtually every aspect of our lives. Yet agriculture literacy and trust in the American food system continue to dwindle.

How do we become agriculturally literate to understand the value of agriculture in our lives?

What Is Agricultural Literacy?

"An agriculturally literate person is defined as 'one who understands and can communicate the source and value of agriculture as it affects our quality of life,'" according to the National Agriculture in the Classroom Organization.[5]

What Do We Know about Agriculture?

The USDA encourages educators and club and community leaders to integrate agricultural concepts and agricultural literacy to teach science, technology, mathematics, reading, writing, social studies, and other subjects in agricultural programs. This chapter will discuss the importance of agriculture literacy and the impact of a warming world on food production. This chapter also highlights how a large number of U.S. schools are employing K–12 gardens in their agriculture education programs.

The Need to Be Agriculturally Literate

It is important for all of us to know more about the value of agriculture—to become agriculturally literate in our quality of life.

According to the American Farm Bureau Foundation for Agriculture (AFBA), "An agriculturally literate person understands how the agricultural industry works—not just where food comes from, but who grows it, agriculture's effect on the economy, environment, technology, lifestyle, and its relationship to livestock."[6]

AFBA also reports that a majority of Americans do not have a basic understanding where their food, fiber, and fuel comes from. The solution to this problem is education.

The AFBA's mission is to increase agricultural literacy among educators, students, and the general public. Their mission is to build awareness and understanding of agriculture through education. The foundation also develops and distributes educational resources, curriculum materials, and programs. The programs provide an excellent understanding of agriculture's importance and its role in our daily lives. One of the programs is the Pillars of Agriculture Literacy.

The Pillars of Agricultural Literacy is a tool designed for people who are planning and developing agricultural literacy programs and initiatives. The tool is useful for educators applying agriculture learning events in the classroom and for alignment to educational standards.

Research at AFBA shows that school gardens have a positive impact on student learning, health, and nutrition. Students learn about good eating habits, science, math, and even some business skills.

Agricultural Literacy in the Classroom

The National Agricultural Literacy Outcomes (NALOs) is another program designed to improve agricultural literacy among K–12 students.[7] The NALO is a set of benchmarks that outline the knowledge, skills, and attitudes students should have to understand and engage with agriculture. The benchmarks assist educators to integrate agricultural concepts into their curriculum, and to provide for a better understanding of agriculture's role in society.

School Gardens: A Little History

Since the 1900s, U.S. school gardens have made major contributions, accomplishments, and much impact in the life story of American culture and history. In 1906, the U.S. Department of Agriculture (USDA) estimated that there were 72,000 school gardens in the United States. The gardeners included teachers, parents, students, and members of the community.

Victory Gardens: World War II

During World War II, Victory Gardens were planted by families in the United States to prevent food shortages. The Victory Garden program increased the production and consumption of fresh vegetables and fruits by more and better home, school, and community gardens to the end that we became a stronger and healthier nation, reported by the U.S. Department of Agriculture.[8]

Some of the goals of the WWII Victory Garden program included:

1. "Increase the production and consumption of fresh vegetables and fruits by more home, school, and community gardens to the end that we become a stronger and healthier nation."
2. "Encourage the proper storage and preservation of surplus from such gardens for distribution and use by families producing it, local school lunches, welfare agencies, and for local emergency food needs."

School Gardens: The Present

In 2023, 2.7 million students were in classroom agriculture programs. Schools used agriculture as a context for science, social studies, and nutrition education content for K–12 classrooms.

School gardens come in all shapes and sizes, and districts with varying amounts of land are finding ways to establish gardens both within and beyond school grounds. Gardens can be as simple as a few containers on a windowsill or can cover many acres, and gardens can thrive in all climates. The school gardens help children gain familiarity and comfort with the fruits and vegetables they see and eat at lunchtime.

Other Benefits from School Garden Programs

- Students learn about where food really comes from. No, not from the grocery store.
- The garden offers opportunities to teach life skills such as gardening and cooking.
- Garden experiences reinforce classroom curriculum and offer opportunities to integrate curricula across many subject areas.
- Gardens provide opportunities for community involvement, a link with friends, neighbors, farmers, volunteers, parents, and community businesses.
- School gardens can grow vegetables to donate to local food pantries. Neighbors who do not have easy access to grocery stores can also benefit from school garden donations.

Diets and Nutrition: School Gardens Grow Healthy Foods

Childhood obesity is a major problem in the United States. Approximately fourteen million children and adolescents suffer from obesity and poor health.

According to the U.S. Department of Agriculture (USDA), many unhealthy eating habits can be established during childhood, which has likely contributed to the current obesity health problems.

Many advocates believe that school gardens will help curb the current obesity trends. According to the National Farm to School Network, "Access to fresh, healthy foods and nutrition education is key to improving children's health."[9]

School garden programs can provide opportunities for students to eat a healthy, nutritious diet while working in the garden. Gardens can teach students about food systems and nutrition. As an example, a garden's health and nutrition program can connect students to lifelong healthy eating habits. These experiences can increase a student's preference for nutritious fruits and vegetables. As they learn, students can start to make the connection between how foods grow, proper diets, and nutrition. School gardening activities, combined with physical activities, may improve childhood dietary intake and prevent overweight and obesity, as well.

Slow Food USA

Slow Food USA is a National School Garden Program (NSGP).[10] The goal of the Slow Food School Garden Network is to support educators and volunteers to become more effective in sustaining nourishing foods in their school garden programs. Slow Food USA's School Garden Network aims to reconnect youth with their food by teaching them how to grow, cook, and enjoy real food—and to have children become more active participants in selecting healthy food choices. Slow Food USA, in partnership with Whole Kids Foundation, has developed a toolkit to help school district food services safely bring school garden produce onto the cafeteria.

School Gardens Can Help Mitigate Climate Change

School gardens can help reduce climate change. By using sustainable farming skills, students can learn how to conserve natural resources, reduce waste, and preserve the environment in the garden ecosystem.

School Gardens Can Help Reduce Climate Change

School garden programs emphasize sustainable farming practices to grow crops. School gardens allow students several ways to protect their environment. Some examples follow.

Many schools use no-dig gardens. There is no tilling or breaking up of the fertile soil. The carbon in the soil provides nutrients to plants and improves water retention. Therefore, keeping the carbon in the ground is critical to maintain healthy soils.

School garden programs use natural fertilizers. They include mulching, composting, and cover crops that gradually fertilize the ground as they break down. Mulch reduces water loss from soil, so there is less time spent watering the garden.

Compost is used to fertilize and enrich soils for improved plant growth. Students use cover crops to cover the soil after harvesting—cover crops such as clovers, buckwheat, ryegrass, and oats. The cover crops also prevent erosion from heavy rainfall.

Many school gardens have also included planting trees in and around the garden. The leafy trees help reduce soil erosion caused by falling rain and improve air quality. The air is less polluted.

Plan and Grow a Victory Climate Garden

Today's students need to be informed about how to grow food in a changing climate. One organization, the Green America Organization, has a program called a Victory Climate Garden. Based in Washington, DC, the program provides beginning gardeners and seasoned gardeners with plans and tips to grow Victory Climate Gardens. The plans include what plants to grow, and when and how to plant them. The Victory Climate Gardens are part of the climate solution—a solution that restores soil health and draws down carbon. The garden soil is used to capture carbon and to grow healthy crops. In the garden, students explore how to use mulch to protect soil, and conserve and store water in rain barrels.[11]

School Gardens Can Monitor School Waste, Too

K–12 schools have a role in educating the next generation about the importance of food conservation and to monitor school waste.

The best way to cut down on food waste is to encourage students to consume what they choose and eat. This involves good planning by school nutrition staff, getting students involved in decision making, and having teachers educate students on the impacts of wasted food.

School gardens can monitor school waste, too. Thirty percent of the world's food is wasted. By growing food, students can learn how much care and time goes into producing fruits and to reduce waste. Adding a composting system to a school garden helps teach children about the decomposition process and eliminating food waste. Thus, gardening is a great opportunity for differentiated instruction as there's something for every student at every skill level.

The following is a short list of some U.S. school gardens.

U.S. School Gardens

Presently there are thousands of school gardens across the United States. As mentioned earlier, the gardens may come in many designs and arrangements. They range from a collection of container flower gardens, to raised vegetable beds, to a half-acre of plowed land. Some schools have indoor garden programs, too. Indoor farming requires no soil. To grow, the plants get all their nutrients from aeroponics, hydroponics, and aquaponics systems. Inside, the LED (light-emitting diode) bulbs provide photosynthesis for plant growth.

"More than 60,000 teachers in 43 states were trained to incorporate agriculture into their lesson plans," asserts Debra Spielmaker, National Agriculture in the Classroom project director. "These teachers in turn engaged with 6.5 million students reported by the states who conduct teacher professional development surveys."[12]

School gardens allow young people to explore how food is grown while they plant, grow, and harvest a variety of fruits and vegetables. These programs also help students develop environmental stewardship and civic pride while they learn.

Berkeley, California: The Edible Schoolyard Project. Alice Waters is a chef, author, food activist, and the founder and owner of Chez Panisse Restaurant in Berkeley, California. She founded the Edible Schoolyard Project in 1995. Today, the Edible Schoolyard is at Dr. Martin Luther King, Jr. Middle School in Berkeley, California.[13] The Edible Schoolyard Project uses organic school gardens, kitchens, and cafeterias to teach both academic subjects and the values of nourishment, stewardship, and community.

The Edible Schoolyard (ESY) includes gardening and cooking for several grades. The program is fully integrated into the programs of the school and provides academic experience for every student. The kitchen staff uses fresh crops to prepare meals for public school students across the city. Through growing, processing, cooking, eating, studying, and even thinking about food, students develop skills, knowledge, and behaviors that enrich their academic and nonacademic lives.

The Alice Waters Institute hosts national and regional gatherings consisting of regenerative-organic farmers, educators, policymakers, philanthropists, nonprofit, and academic. In 2025, the Edible Schoolyard Project hosted Climate Food Hope at the Smithsonian in Washington, DC, as well as Earth Day and Climate Week events in California and New York.

New York, New York: Green Bronx Machine, Stephen Ritz. The Green Bronx Machine was started with the collaboration between an educator, Stephen Ritz, and his students. The Green Bronx Machine has evolved into a K-12+ model fully integrated into a core curriculum.[14]

Ritz and his students have grown more than 100,000 pounds of vegetables in the South Bronx. The program has also improved school attendance and provided thousands of youth jobs in the Bronx.

The Green Bronx Machine curriculum includes videos and resources and is used in hundreds of schools across the United States and internationally. The schools are in Colombia, Dubai, Cairo, and Doha, the capital city in Qatar.

In 2024, Ritz brought programming to more than 120 new schools across the United States. The Green Bronx Machine expanded partnerships with Babylon Micro-Farms, Southwest Foodservice for Excellence, and We Are Teachers.

Denver, Colorado: Slow Food Denver, Youth Farm Stands. The Youth Farm Stand (YFS) is a single-vendor market on school grounds that is run by the students of that school. Located in Denver, the Youth Farm Stands can be used to teach nutrition and healthy eating.[15]

Using the school-based farm stand, the school sells freshly harvested produce from their school garden. The stand can also sell produce from local farms and gardens. The YFS model is adaptable to the needs and resources of the school and community. The farm stand can supply fresh produce for neighborhoods lacking healthy food. The school gardens allow students to be participants in a local food supply chain by growing food for the salad bars in the cafeteria. The school gardens can also grow food for local food pantries to feed the hungry families in the community.

Harvests from the garden are prepared in portable kitchens by local chefs. Working in the kitchen, students learn how to prepare food with simple recipes. Students discover the taste of freshly picked produce.

Nevada. The Green Our Planet is located in Las Vegas and operates the largest school garden and hydroponics program in the United States. Students in pre-K to twelfth grade can learn about a variety of subjects including STEM, nutrition, and conservation. Or they can learn about STEAM (science, technology, engineering, art, and math), nutrition and conservation through project-based learning.

In 2013, Green Our Planet launched its Outdoor Garden Classroom. The Outdoor Garden program helps public and private schools raise funding for outdoor school gardens. Green Our Planet helps schools establish outdoor school gardens, hydroponics, and nutrition programs throughout the United States.

Schools in their hydroponics program receive everything they need to have a successful garden. Each school receives the materials for six different kinds of hydroponics units. Lettuce, chard, tomatoes, peppers, cucumbers, and strawberries are among the many fruits and vegetables that grow in the hydroponic system.

Chicago, Illinois. Big Green has built two hundred Learning Gardens in Chicago since 2012. The Learning Garden is a teaching tool for students to learn about healthy food. Those two hundred Chicago Learning Garden Schools include 125,000 students who have participated and more than four hundred teachers who were trained in one school year.[16] The Learning Gardens provide families, teachers, and schools with at-home resources, remote training, curriculum, and access to real food to ensure no child misses out on a high-quality education each year.

They are working with their partners to invite special guests, experts in garden and food education, to provide some new and inspiring content to support bringing the garden and cooking experiences into the virtual classroom.

North Dakota. The Cannon Ball Elementary School Garden is located on the Standing Rock Sioux reservation in North Dakota. The Standing Rock Sioux Reservation is situated in North Dakota and South Dakota. Through a partnership with NDSU Sioux County Extension/4-H, the students participate in hands-on, outdoor activities in growing food in the community gardens. They engage in STEM activities, attend 4-H camps, and participate in leadership activities and school enrichment programs. The garden not only promotes a healthy lifestyle; it improves the students' behavior and performance at school and develops their appreciation for the environment.[17]

Arizona: Navajo Reservation, Tuba City Primary School. At Navajo Reservation Arizona, the Tuba City Primary School serves produce grown in its school garden for cafeteria meals. The first certified school garden on an Arizona reservation means healthy local produce for kids. The Johns Hopkins Center for American Indian Health (JHCAIH) operates the Edible School Garden Program at the Tuba City Primary School as a part of its community-based gardening and farming initiative. Now that the school garden is certified, children can enjoy the produce they grow in their school garden at lunch. The first harvest of the 2015 growing season brought red and green lettuce onto the lunch trays of smiling kindergartners through third graders. As the growing season progresses, the volume of produce will increase and the 140 square meters (1,500 square feet) garden provides a variety of vegetables for students to incorporate into their daily lunches. Garden produce will be available to children throughout the summer through summer school programming. An on-campus high tunnel creates the environment needed to grow greens during colder winter months.[18]

Newark, New Jersey: Philip's Academy Charter. At Philip's Academy Charter, in Newark, New Jersey, the public charter school raises both an aeroponic farm and a rooftop garden. Each grade has a grade-level garden plot in which teachers and students plant fruits and/or vegetables.

The school also has a test kitchen used by students to cook the produce they grow. The students plant, water, and care for garden beds of carrots, spinach, and radishes as well as a host of other fruits and vegetables. That aims to encourage healthy eating. In the garden, the school integrates gardening activities with core math, science, art, language arts, health and physical education, and social studies.

North Carolina: Growing Minds. Growing Minds is the farm-to-school program of the Appalachian Sustainable Agriculture Project (ASAP), a nonprofit based in Asheville, North Carolina. The project serves western North Carolina and bordering states. Growing Minds was one of the first programs of its kind in the country. The program started in 2002 at Hazelwood Elementary in Haywood County, North Carolina. The program now provides support for several counties. In 2023, Growing Minds trained and/or provided resources for farm-to-school programming to more than 1,000 educators and 20,000 children. The children range in age from early childhood through high school! Growing Minds trains individuals to establish farm-to-school gardens and to integrate gardening into state and national curricula. They emphasize how to sustain a garden program by involving community partners, such as parents, farmers, college students, and agricultural professionals. The gardeners grow a variety of food that include blueberries, broccoli, carrots, green beans, mushrooms, peppers, radishes, sugar snap peas, sweet corn, and watermelons. And students will eat what they grow![19]

Tyler, Texas: Micro Family Farms. Mike Loggins is the founder of Micro Family Farms. The Micro Family school garden programs provide educational enrichment and nutritional benefit for students throughout the entire school year The farm grows about seventy different kinds of vegetables for twelve months out of the year. Seasonal vegetables include lettuces, strawberries, kale, collards, arugula, herbs, and more! The Farm Academy brings the pleasure of harvesting and eating fresh vegetables to students, teachers, and school family. The school is focusing on leafy greens that the school's chef can work into soups, to deliver the maximum nutritional content.[20]

Philadelphia, Pennsylvania: Francis Scott Key School. Francis Scott Key School is a public elementary school located in the Central South Philadelphia neighborhood.[21] The Key School garden was designed and built by students in the South Philadelphia High School carpentry program. Construction was completed in June 2015. The garden has four garden beds. In the raised beds, students grow perennials such as a rose and butterfly bush. The garden also has native pollinator plants including milkweed, black-eyed Susan, and bee balm. Spring and summer bulbs bloom every year as well as fruits, herbs, and vegetables that are planted yearly. Students are growing vegetables and learning about food preparation.

Students in the Community Club explore gardens and make observations of plant life. In a sunny spot, they can view bee balm, chives, and a rose bush beginning to sprout. Students in the Community Club plant native flowers (echinacea and New England aster). In the future, more metal raised garden beds and flexible seating will be built.

To wrap up this chapter, I wanted to include another school garden. No, not in the United States. Well, where? In the most populated country in the world: *India*. India has kitchen gardens in all of their schools.

India

India Requires All Schools to Have Kitchen Gardens

The Ministry of Human Resource Development (MHRD) in India has issued guidelines to all schools in the country for setting up School Nutrition Gardens (also called Kitchen Gardens). The population of India is more than 1.4 billion, the largest population in the world.

The gardens will provide students with places to learn about growing and to grow their own food. The goal is to teach all students in India that growing is independent, and possible even in a crowded urban environment. The guidelines also suggest that students learn to appreciate all parts of a fruit and vegetable, and other ways to "think outside the box."

Krishi Vigyan Kendras in India are "farm science centers" where farmers and university scientists collaborate. These centers include the Department of Agriculture/Horticulture, Food and Nutrition Boards, agriculture universities, and the Forest Department. All of them supply students with seeds, saplings, manure, as well as training and technical assistance to create School Nutrition Gardens.

Schools in urban areas throughout India are encouraged to grow fruits and vegetables in pots on terraces or rooftops, or to grow plants that will climb walls and need a minimal amount of space. Students will be responsible for managing the gardens with their teachers' help.

The MHRD guidelines suggest that every class should spend one or two hours per week in their school's garden. Additionally, school eco clubs (which focus on improving environmental conditions) should be established to provide extra opportunities for students and their parents to become involved in planting and cultivating fruits and vegetables.

The food grown in school nutrition gardens can be incorporated into school meals. School cooks will be encouraged to engage in cooking competitions to create innovative and tasty dishes featuring items grown by the students.

Gardening is a sustainable and inexpensive way for individuals to access healthy foods. Instituting kitchen gardens in every school in the country can teach children how to grow their own food. Furthermore, studies have shown that when children grow their own food they are more likely to eat it and bring healthy eating behaviors back to their families.[22]

CONCLUSION: AGRICULTURE IS FACING MANY CHALLENGES

By 2050, the world's population will be more than 9.5 billion. By that time farmers may be required to almost double the amount of crops that are harvested today. Problems? In the future, growing food, raising livestock, and fishing with the same amount of land and water reserves we have today will be a challenge. Floods, wildfires, sea level rise, and droughts will continue to impact food production.

Agriculture is also a major contributor to greenhouse emissions, water pollution, and land degradation. In 2023, Special Presidential Envoy for Climate John Kerry warned that "the world can't tackle climate change without first addressing the agriculture sector's emissions. This sector needs innovation now more than ever."

Feeding the World: How Innovations in Agriculture Are Saving the Planet heard the call for the need of innovations in agriculture, ranching, and fisheries in a warming world.

The chapters present the hard work and service of people and organizations who are employing a wide variety of innovations to grow food while protecting the water, air, land, and wildlife in the agriculture ecosystems. The chapters provide positive and uplifting topics and the technology to mitigate climate change, too.

The innovations reported in the chapters include regenerative farming practices, vertical aeroponic and hydroponic farms, aquaponic and seaweed farming, freight container farms, soilless greenhouses, and protecting the health of farm workers. The agriculture technology (agritech) chapters include hardware, software, robots, drones, drip irrigation, and GPS technology. The future is urban farming and the innovations needed to feed millions living in the cities. The book also enhances the chapters with human interest stories of those who heard the call of service.

The Need to Be Agriculturally Literate

Tomorrow's agriculture depends on today's young people. Today's students need to be informed how to grow food in a warming world climate. Students, as well as all of us, need to be agriculturally literate.

As mentioned previously, most adults and young people know very little about agriculture and its value in their daily lives. It is important for all of us to know more about the value of agriculture—to become agriculturally literate in our quality of life.

As referenced earlier, according to the American Farm Bureau for Agriculture (AFBA), "An agriculturally literate person understands how the agricultural industry works—not just where food comes from, but who grows it, agriculture's effect on the economy, environment, technology, lifestyle, and its relationship to livestock."

The USDA invites educators and club and community leaders to assimilate agricultural concepts and agricultural literacy to teach science, technology, mathematics, reading, writing, social studies, and other subjects in agricultural and school garden programs.

School garden programs increase student agricultural literacy and climate literacy. Gardens can teach students about food systems and nutrition. As an example, a garden's health and nutrition program can connect students to lifelong healthy eating habits. These experiences can increase a student's preference for nutritious fruits and vegetables. As they learn, students can start to make the connection between how foods grow, proper diets, and nutrition. School garden programs emphasize sustainable farming practices to grow crops. As an example, maintaining healthy soils in a school garden can reduce greenhouse gases, such as carbon dioxide (CO_2), being emitted into the atmosphere.

As we look into the future, we need to inspire our young people who, hopefully, will be more involved in being energy efficient, exploring hands-on innovative farm projects, and investigating careers in agriculture vocations. The motivation to inspire them to reach the goal, in most cases, lies in the hands of their teachers, communities, mentors, peers, and of course their parents.

APPENDIX 1
Farm Bureaus, Associations, Administrations, and Businesses

American Farm Bureau

The American Farm Bureau Federation is the Voice of Agriculture®. We are farm and ranch families working together to build a sustainable future of safe and abundant food, fiber, and renewable fuel for our nation and the world.
 600 Maryland Avenue SW, Suite 1000, Washington D.C. 20024

Black Urban Growers Association

The Black Urban Growers Association maintains a network and community support in order to foster Black leadership in food and farm advocacy. Their programs include the Black Farmers & Urban Gardeners Conference, a national conference started in 2010 that brings together Black farmers, advocates, chefs, and communities to share their best practices and leadership efforts.
 1350 Broadway, Suite 201. New York, NY 10018

Environmental Protection Agency (EPA)

Understanding and addressing climate change is critical to EPA's mission of protecting human health and the environment. EPA tracks and reports greenhouse gas emissions, leverages, and sound science to combat climate change. EPA provides resources for educators to help students learn about climate change and how it impacts the world around them.
 1200 Pennsylvania Avenue NW. Washington, DC 20460

Feeding America

Feeding America is the largest charity working to end hunger in the United States. We partner with food banks, food pantries, and local food programs to bring food to people facing hunger. We advocate for policies that create long-term solutions to hunger. Feeding America is a nationwide network of 200 food banks and 60,000 food pantries and meal programs fighting to end hunger. The organization provides assistance to one in seven Americans, including 12 million children.

61 North Clark Street, Suite 700. Chicago, IL 60601

Food and Agriculture Organization of the United Nations (FAO)

The FAO is a specialized agency of the United Nations that works to achieve food security for all. The FAO works in over 130 countries worldwide, working toward goals to set international standards for food safety and justice, eradicate food and water related diseases around the world, and limit global hunger.

Headquarters in Rome, Italy

National Aeronautics and Space Administration (NASA)

NASA uses its platform of exciting missions and world-class experts to aid in building a skilled STEM workforce with the technical skills needed to carry forward our nation's vital work in aeronautics and space into the future.

300 Hidden Figures Way SW, Washington, D.C.

National Farmers Union NFU

NFU was founded by ten family farmers in 1902 as the Farmers Educational Cooperative Union of America in Point, Texas. The National Farmers Union Mission is to advocate for family farmers, ranchers, and their communities through education, cooperation, and legislation.

20 F Street NW, Suite 300. Washington, DC 20001

National Nanotechnology Initiative (NNI)

The vision of the National Nanotechnology Initiative (NNI) is a future in which the ability to understand and control matter at the nanoscale leads to ongoing revolutions in technology and industry that benefit society.
2415 Eisenhower Avenue, Alexandria, VA 22314

National Oceanic and Atmospheric Administration (NOAA)

The NOAA's mission is to better understand our natural world and help protect its precious resources extends beyond national borders to monitor global weather and climate, and work with partners around the world.
1401 Constitution Avenue NW, Room 5128, Washington, DC 20230

National Young Farmers Coalition NYFC

The NYFC is working to halt and even reverse the decline of family farming in the U.S. by representing, mobilizing, and engaging young farmers. We are working for comprehensive climate legislation and administrative action that provides resources to the young farmers and farmers of color who are and will combat climate change and build resiliency on their farms across the country.
418 Broadway, Albany, NY 12207

ReFED

ReFED is a data-driven guide for businesses, government, funders, and nonprofits to collectively reduce food waste at scale. In 2023, 31% of all food in the U.S. goes unsold or uneaten—and most of that ends up as waste. That is equivalent to 24 percent of landfill methane and landfill volume.

Explore ReFED Resources Library. Their report represents a landscape assessment across the food waste ecosystem.
122 S. Michigan Ave., Suite 1390-L74, Chicago, IL 60603

The Regenerative Agriculture Alliance

The Regenerative Agriculture Alliance was created in 2018 as the non-profit arm of a larger ecosystem designed to build a regenerative, equitable, and socially just agriculture sector.
301 Division Street S., Northfield, MN 55057

Rodale Institute

Rodale Institute is a nonprofit conducting independent research to uncover and share regenerative organic farming The Rodale Institute gathers research, farmer training, and consumer education to push the organic movement around the world. Regenerative organic agriculture not only maintains resources but improves them.
611 Siegfriedale Road, Kutztown, PA 19530-9749

Soil Health Institute

The Soil Health Institute is a nonprofit whose mission is to safeguard and enhance the vitality and productivity of soils through scientific research and advancement. The Institute works with many partners to conduct and translate soil health science into action that benefits farmers, the environment, and society.
2803 Slater Road, Suite 115, Morrisville, NC 27560

The Forever Green Initiative

The Forever Green Initiative is developing and improving winter-hardy annual and perennial crops that protect soil and water while driving new economic opportunities for growers, industry, and communities across Minnesota. Minnesota has 27 million acres of farmland, occupying nearly half the 55.6 million acres in the state.
224 McNamara Alumni Center, University of Minnesota, 200 Oak St. S.E., Minneapolis, MN 55455

APPENDIX 1

The Land Institute

The Land Institute is a global movement for perennial, diverse, truly regenerative agriculture at scale. The Land Institute's goal is to create an agriculture system that mimics natural systems to produce ample food and reduce or eliminate the negative impacts of agriculture.

2440 E Water Well Rd., Salina, Kansas 67401

United States Department of Agriculture

When President Lincoln established the United States Department of Agriculture, he called it the "People's Department." At USDA people are working to be a model department that serves all people of our great Nation. The National Agricultural Library (NAL) is one of five national libraries of the United States. It houses one of the world's largest collections devoted to agriculture and its related sciences.

1400 Independence Ave., SW Washington, DC 20250

World Bank Group

The World Bank Group's mission is to end extreme poverty and boost shared prosperity on a livable planet. Climate-smart agriculture (CSA) is an integrated approach to managing landscapes—cropland, livestock, forests and fisheries–that address the interlinked challenges of food security and climate change.

1818 H Street NW, Washington, DC 20433

YieldWise

In 2016, The Rockefeller Foundation launched YieldWise with the goal of demonstrating how the world can halve food loss by 2030, one of the UN's Sustainable Development Goals. It is the first global solution to food loss and waste that works across the entire food system: from farm to store to table and beyond.

Headquarters in Washington, DC

For more information about GPS Official U.S. government information about the Global Positioning System (GPS) and related topics https://www.gps.gov

For additional information on the Guide to Measuring Household Food Security. Contact the United States Department of Agriculture, ers.usda.gov/.

VIDEO RESOURCES

AMNH; Amazing Ice Cores: 150,000 Years of Climate History. Follow scientist-adventurer Lonnie Thompson to the 5,670-meter-high Quelccaya ice cap in the Peruvian Andes.

Earth Has a Fever. To review conditions of global warming refer to a NASA video. *NASA's Earth Minute: Earth Has a Fever.* Data from NASA's global network of satellites, airborne missions and surface monitoring systems is used to build climate models that help us understand the causes and effects of global warming. Go to: https://www.jpl.nasa.gov/edu/learn/video/nasas-earth-minute-earth-has-a-fever/. Source: National Aeronautics and Space Administration (NASA) Jet Propulsion Laboratory, Pasadena, California.

Climate Changes Affects Community Health. Climate change, together with other natural and human-made health stressors, influences human health and disease in numerous ways. These videos present the challenges of climate-related changes such as more frequent episodes of extreme heat, storms, and flooding; poor air quality, and the spread of disease—and how we can address those changes. Centers for Disease Control and Prevention. Go to: http://cdc.gov/climateandhealth/videos.html

You Tube. Inside World's Biggest & Most Advanced Vertical Farm

Aeroponic Systems Use NASA Aeroponics to Grow Food. Go to: https://www.youtube.com/watch?v=m6o5LTl6GJw

The Circle Food. Find out more about how this farm uses aquaponics. Go to: The Corporate: The Circle Food and Energy Solutions. https://www.youtube.com/watch?v=ShWU7IgGq7Q&t=93s

APPENDIX 2
A Condensed History of American Agriculture 1800–2000

This timeline highlights important developments in American agriculture over the past two hundred years, focusing on major changes, key legislation, and shifts in government policy. It should offer high school and college readers valuable insights into the evolution of agriculture in the United States while keeping the information concise and easy to understand.

Pre-1800
1748: Jared Eliot, a minister and doctor in Killingworth, Connecticut, writes a book on agriculture to improve crops and to conserve soil.
1789: The U.S. Constitution goes into effect. The federal government's enumerated powers do not include the creation of farm and food subsidy programs.

1800–1819
1810: First U.S. agriculture periodical published.

1820–1839
1820: The House of Representatives creates an agriculture committee.
1824: Solomon and William Drown of Providence, Rhode Island publish *Farmer's Guide*, which discusses erosion and its causes and remedies.
1826: Agriculture Committee established—U.S. Senate.
1834: McCormick Reaper popularized.

1840–1859
1840: The first Census of Agriculture is completed.
1849: Department of Interior is established.
1850: More factory-grade agriculture products become available on the market, increasing productivity but putting more pressure on farmers for upfront capital expenses.

1860–1879
1862: The U.S. Department of Agriculture is established. President Abraham Lincoln calls it the "people's department."

1862: The Morrill Act provides grants of federal land to the states. The states are to use the proceeds of land sales to create colleges focused on agricultural studies.
1874: Proliferation of barbed wire ends the era of unrestricted, free open-range grazing.

1880–1899
1881: Congress establishes a Division of Forestry in the USDA.
1887: The Hatch Act provides subsidies to the states for agriculture research.
1891: The Forest Reserve Act allows presidents to set aside forest reserves out of public lands. These reserves are managed by the Department of the Interior.

1900–1919
1900: There are eleven million Americans employed on farms and 2,900 employed by the USDA. A century later, there are three million employed on farms and 105,000 employed by the USDA.
1905: The Federal Forest Transfer Act moves control of the forest reserves from the Department of the Interior to the USDA's new Forest Service.
1905: Major scandal hits the USDA when an employee seeking personal gain leaks advance cotton market information to a speculator.
1911: The Weeks Act authorizes federal subsidies to the states for forest fire prevention, and it allows the Forest Service to purchase private lands for national forests.
1914: The USDA opens state and regional offices across the country.
1914: The Smith-Lever Act begins subsidies to the land-grant colleges for agricultural research.
1916: The Federal Farm Loan Act creates cooperative "land banks" to provide loans to farmers. Legislation during the 1930s expands this Farm Credit System, and today the FCS is a fifty-state network of financial cooperatives with assets of $90 billion.

1920–1939
1929: The Agricultural Marketing Act creates the Federal Farm Board to subsidize agricultural cooperatives.
1929: The Federal Reserve System precipitates the Great Depression by allowing the U.S. money supply to shrink by one-third between 1929 and 1933. Agricultural commodity prices fall even more than general prices, which puts farmers in a squeeze.
1933: The Agricultural Adjustment Act, and subsequent New Deal laws, create the forerunners of today's major farm subsidy programs. The main thrust of the AAA is to limit production to raise commodity prices.
1935: USDA employment more than triples between 1929 and 1935, reaching 85,000. USDA employment reaches 100,000 by 1958 and peaks at 138,000 in 1978.

1940–1959
1946: The National School Lunch Act creates a permanent subsidy program to provide food to schools, building on the surplus commodities program of 1935.
1947: General Agreement on Tariffs and Trade (GATT) is established.
1949: A new Agriculture Adjustment Act extends crop price support and subsidy policies, adding subsidies for the dairy industry and putting farm programs into permanent law.

APPENDIX 2

1960–1979

1964: The Food Stamp Act creates what has become one of the largest welfare programs, a program that is known for major fraud and abuse. The program currently costs federal taxpayers more than $35 billion a year.

1973: With soaring prices for agricultural commodities, the mid-1970s would have been a good time to end farm programs. Instead, the farm bills of 1973 and 1977 take a business-as-usual subsidy approach.

1985: Despite the Reagan administration's proposals to cut farm subsidies, the poor shape of farm finances during the 1980s prompts Congress to pass the expensive Food Security Act of 1985.

1980–2009

1996: Congress changes course in farm policy with the passage of the Federal Agriculture Improvement and Reform Act—the "Freedom to Farm" law. The law is designed to allow farmers greater planting flexibility and better align producer decisions with market supply and demand.

2002: The Farm Security and Rural Investment Act reverts to old-style subsidy increases and price supports as farm-state politicians reject the modest reform proposals of the Bush administration.

2008: The Food, Conservation, and Energy Act expands farm subsidies, and it is enacted over a presidential veto.

NOTES

Introduction

1. See https://www.washingtonpost.com/news/wonk/wp/2017/06/15/seven-percent-of-americans-think-chocolate-milk-comes-from-brown-cows-and-thats-not-even-the-scary-part/.
2. Patty McGinnis, ed., "From the Editor's Desk: Developing ag Literacy," *Science Scope*, July 2019.
3. World Wildlife Fund, "Climate," https://www.worldwildlife.org/pages/climate.
4. Special Presidential Envoy for Climate John Kerry, "John Kerry Targets Agriculture as Part of the Climate Crisis," Fox News, May 10, 2023.

Chapter 1

1. Food and Agriculture Organization (FAO), *How to Feed the World in 2050*, fao.org, October 2009.
2. Tom Vilsack, USDA address, October 24, 2011.
3. "Climate Change Threatens the World's Food Supply, United Nations Warns," *New York Times*, August 8, 2019.
4. National Oceanic and Atmospheric Administration (NOAA), 2025, https://www.noaa.gov/news/2024-was-worlds-warmest-year-on-record.
5. National Aeronautics and Space Administration (NASA), 2025, https://www.usa.gov/agencies/national-aeronautics-and-space-administration.
6. National Oceanic and Atmospheric Association (NOAA), National Climate Data Center, 2025, https://www.noaa.gov/news/2024-was-worlds-warmest-year-on-record.
7. Pew Research Center surveys, 2025, https://www.pewresearch.org/u-s-surveys/.
8. NASA's Jet Propulsion Laboratory, 2025, *Ice Cores*, https://science.nasa.gov/science-research/earth-science/climate-science/core-questions-an-introduction-to-ice-cores/.
9. American Farm Bureau Federation, *Major Disasters and Severe Weather Caused Damages of Crops and Rangelands*, February 29, 2024, https://www.fb.org/market-

NOTES

intel/major-disasters-and-severe-weather-caused-over-21-billion-in-crop-losses-in-2023.

10 UN Development Programme, *A 2016 Study on Climate Change in Mexico*, 2016, https://www.adaptation-undp.org/explore/latin-america-and-caribbean/mexico.

11 UN Environment Programme (UNEP), 2025, *Climate Change Caused Caucasus Glaciers to Retreat 600 Meters, Shrinking Freshwater Supplies*. https://www.unep.org.

12 National Oceanic and Atmospheric Association (NOAA), *NOAA Fisheries Climate Science Strategy and Objectives*, 2025, https://www.fisheries.noaa.gov/national/climate/noaa-fisheries-climate-science-strategy.

13 U.S. Geological Survey(USGS), *Sea Level Rise Can Infiltrate into Fresh Groundwater Supplies*, 2025, https://www.usgs.gov/centers/woods-hole-coastal-and-marine-science-center/science/science-topics/sea-level-rise.

14 California Department of Forestry and Fire Protection (CalFire), *All-Hazard Response for Floods, Fires, Earthquakes and Other Disasters*, 2025, https://www.fire.ca.gov.

15 The European Forest Fire Information System (EFFIS), provides updated information on wildfires in Europe; https://forest-fire.emergency.copernicus.eu.

16 Nature Food is a monthly online journal publishing original research, reviews, comments, and opinions on the theme of food; https://www.nature.com/natfood/.

17 Honor Eldridge, "What Does a Global Pandemic Mean for a Global Food System?," *Resilience*, April 29, 2020.

18 USDA, Economic Research Service (ERS), 2025, https://www.ers.usda.gov.

Chapter 2

1 World Bank, *Climate-Smart Agriculture*, 2025. The World Bank Group is a leading financier of agriculture. https://www.worldbank.org/ext/en/who-we-are.

2 Intergovernmental Panel on Climate Change (IPCC), *Greenhouse Gases Emissions*, 2022. IPCC assesses the science related to climate change. https://www.ipcc.ch.

3 Bill Gates, *How to Avoid a Climate Disaster: The Solutions We Have and the Breakthroughs We Need* (New York, Toronto: Alfred A. Knopf, 2021).

4 U.S. Environmental Protection Agency (EPA), *Preventing Animal Waste from Contaminating Surface and Groundwater*, 2025, https://www.epa.gov.

5 USDA's Natural Resources Conservation Service, *Manure Management*, 2025, https://www.nrcs.usda.gov/getting-assistance/technical-assistance/manure-and-nutrient-management.

6 One Green Planet, *How Factory Farming Creates Air Pollution*, 2025, https://www.onegreenplanet.org/environment/how-factory-farming-creates-air-pollution/

7 Migrant Clinician Network, *Health Education and Health Justice for Migrant Workers in Their Communities*, 2025, https://www.migrantclinician.org.

8 UN Food and Agriculture Organization (FAO), *Water Pollution from Agriculture*, 2025, https://www.fao.org.

9 National Water Quality Assessment (NAWQA), *Tracking and Forecasting the Nation's Water Quality*, 2025, usgs.gov.

10 U.S. Environmental Protection Agency (EPA), *The Importance of Ground Water and Human Health*, 2025, https://www.epa.gov.

11 *The Guardian*, "More Than Half of South Asia's Groundwater Is Contaminated to Use—Study," March 29, 2016.

12 *Nature*, 2025. Nature is a British weekly international scientific journal. https://www.nature.com.

13 *Smithsonian Magazine*, "Taking a Closer Look at Global Water Shortages," 2025. Mexico City reservoirs are at risk of running out of water. https://www.smithsonianmag.com.

14 *UN World Water Development Report*, 2025. UN-Water's flagship report on water and sanitation issues. https://www.unwater.org.

15 "UN Reports That World Is Off Track on Water and Sanitation Goal," United Nations Report, July 2018.

16 WaterAid, 2025. Millions of people are living without water, toilets, and hygiene. Donations can purchase water tanks and hygiene kits. https://www.wateraid.org.

17 Charlene Ren, founder of MyH20, A Water Information Network, 2025. Xiaoyuan "Charlene" Ren is the founder of MyH2O. Charlene Ren, UN Young Champions of Nature-based Solutions. china.un.org.

18 *National Geographic*, "75 percent of Earth's Land Areas Are Degraded," April 21, 2017, https://www.nationalgeographic.com.

19 Soil Health Institute, *Soil Health is the Foundation for Regenerative Agriculture*, 2025. The Soil Health Institute is advancing agricultural sciences around the globe. https://soilhealthinstitute.org.

20 IPBES, "The Assessment Report on Land Degradation and Restoration Summary for Policymakers," 2018.

21 Forest Declaration Assessment, 2025. The Forest Declaration Dashboard provides users with data and findings on forests, The Forest Declaration Assessment tracks progress to enable accountability to meet the world's 2030 forest goals. https://forestdeclaration.org.

22 REDD+ (UN Framework Convention on Climate Change [UNFCCC]), 2025. REDD+ primarily aims at the implementation of activities by national governments to reduce human pressure on forests that result in greenhouse gas emissions. https://www.un-redd.org.

Chapter 3

1 Tom Vilsack, US Department of Agriculture (USDA), *Our National Security Depends on Feeding a Growing World*, 2011, https://www.usda.gov.

2 World Resources Institute, *How to Manage the Global Land Squeeze*, 2023. https://www.wri.org.

NOTES

3 Eisenhower's address at Bradley University, Peoria, Illinois, September 25, 1956.
4 Forever Green Initiative, 2025. Forever Green crops can help farmers build soil health, profitably. https://www.forevergreen.umn.edu.
5 Crop Swap LA, 2025. Grow food on unused spaces in ways that create jobs, preserve water, and equitably distribute the food. https://www.cropswapla.org.
6 US Department of Agriculture, National Resources Conservation Service, *Conservation at Work: No Till*, 2025. https://www.nrcs.usda.gov.
7 North Central Sustainable Agriculture Research and Education (SARE), 2025. Cover crops can slow erosion, improve soil, and smother weeds. https://northcentral.sare.org.
8 Environmental Protection Agency, *Integrated Pest Management*, 2024. Farmers identify their pests before spraying. https://www.epa.gov/.
9 USDA, Natural Resources Conservation Service, *Drip Irrigation*, 2025. https://www.nrcs.usda.gov.
10 The Water Project, *Sand Dams*, 2024. Capturing the water where it falls is essential for improving environments. https://thewaterproject.org/sand-dams.
11 US Department of Agriculture (USDA), *Agroforestry*, 2023. Agroforestry combines agriculture and forestry technologies.
12 Food and Agriculture Organization (FAO), *System of Rice Intensification*, 2013. Jesuit Father Henri de Laulanié in Madagascar. https://www.fao.org.
13 US Department of Agriculture (USDA), *Characteristics and Influential Factors of Food Deserts*, 2025. Food access and store proximity, food retailing and marketing, and food prices. https://www.ers.usda.gov.
14 Melinda Cater, "Health Benefits of Farmers Markets," John Hopkins Medicine, hopkinsmedicine.org.

Chapter 4

1 U.S. Department of Agriculture (USDA), National Institute of Food and Agriculture, *Importance of Agricultural Technology*, 2025, https://www.nifa.usda.gov.
2 U.S. Department of Agriculture (USDA), Economic Research Service, 2024. Variable rate technology adoption is on the rise. https://ers.usda.gov/.
3 AeroVironment, Inc, Quantix™ Mapper, 2025, https://draganfly.com.
4 Agritecture, *DLI for Daily Light Integral*, 2025. How much light do crops need? https://www.agritecture.com.
5 See https://library.ucsc.edu/reg-hist/stephen-r-gliessman-alfred-e-heller-professor-of-agroecology-uc-santa-cruz.
6 Monnit Corporation, *Soil Moisture Sensor*, 2025. The sensor improves irrigation scheduling. https://www.monnit.com.
7 Mordor Intelligence, "Agricultural Robots Market Size and Share," July 2025.

8 Blue River Technology, 2025. LettuceBot 1 is a robot that precisely, if needed, thins lettuce fields. https://www.bluerivertechnology.com.
9 National Aeronautics and Space Administration (NASA), 2025. Airborne Visible/InfraRed Imaging Spectrometer measures light that is reflected off Earth's surface, tracks methane. https://www.nasa.gov.
10 Grassroots Carbon, 2025. PastureMap is an application that ranchers use for grazing management. https://grassrootscarbon.com.
11 National Oceanic and Atmospheric Administration (NOAA) Fisheries, 2025. NOAA Fisheries using saildrones to study fish such as Alaskan pollock. https://www.fisheries.noaa.gov.
12 National Nanotechnological Initiative (NNI), 2025. Nanotechnology applications include water treatment and precision agriculture. https://www.nano.gov.
13 U.S. Department of Agriculture (USDA), Natural Resources Conservation Service, 2025. Virtual fencing allows ranchers to move livestock without physical fences. https://www.nrcs.usda.gov.

Chapter 5

1 Dickson Despommier, *The Vertical Farm: Feeding the World in the 21st Century* (New York: Picador, 2011).
2 Fortune Business Insights, *The Vertical Farming Market Is Growing*, 2025. https://www.fortunebusinessinsights.com.
3 U.S. Department of Agriculture (USDA), 2025. Indoor and vertical farming may be part of the solution to rising demands for food and limited natural resources. https://www.usda.gov/farming.
4 Business Research Company, "Hydroponics Market Overview," 2024.
5 Vertical Harvest Farms, CNN Champions for Change Award, 2025, https://verticalharvestfarms.com.
6 Sheikh Ahmed bin Saeed Al Maktoum, chairman and chief executive, Emirates Airline and Group, 2025, https://www.theemiratesgroup.com.
7 Sky Greens, 2025. Jack Ng, Inventor and Founder of Sky Greens, Singapore. Sky Greens is the world's first low carbon, hydraulic driven vertical farm. https://www.skygreens.com.
8 Robotic vertical farm in Chengdu City, 2023. CGTN is the English-language news channel of state-run China Global Television Network based in Beijing, China. https://news.cgtn.com.
9 Eeden Farms, Nassau, Bahamas, 2025. Eeden Farms is an unfunded company based in Nassau City, founded in 2013. bahamaslocal.com.
10 Agrotonomy, 2025. Rooftop Aeroponic Tower Farm, Paris, France, https://agrotonomy.com.
11 Vegetable Research Laboratory, 2025. Dr. Kai-Shu Ling is a research plant pathologist with the Vegetable Research Laboratory in Charleston, South Carolina. https://www.ars.usda.gov.

NOTES

12 Application Technology Research Unit, 2025. Dr. James Altland is a research horticulturist with the Application Technology Research (ARS) Unit in Wooster, Ohio. ARS is scientific in-house research agency. ARS delivers scientific solutions to national and global agricultural challenges. https://www.ars.usda.gov.

Chapter 6

1   Fortune Business Insights, "Aquaponics Market Size," August 2025.
2   FarmPod, Santa Fe, New Mexico, 2022. Vertical aquaponic food production system. http://www.farminapod.com.
3   Edenworks, 2025. Brooklyn, New York. An aquaponic vertical farm. tracxn.com edenworks.com.
4   Ouroboros Farms, Half Moon Bay, California, 2025. One of the largest commercial aquaponic farms in the United States. https://www.ouroborosfarms.com.
5   Circle Food & Energy Solutions, Rome, Italy, 2025. The aquaponic farm raises Japanese koi fish and vegetables including edible flowers. https://www.thecircle.global/ https://fusionfarms.ag.
6   Fusion Farms, Mayagüez, Puerto Rico, 2024. A vertical aquaponic farm inside a large vacant concrete building.
7   Aquponi-House, 2023. The future of eco-friendly farming. https://waterco.com.sg/case-studies/aquaculture/Aquponi%20House%20Japan.
8   Ronald Osinga, "Seaweed Farms Offer a Sustainable Source of Vegetable Protein," *Smithsonian Magazine*, May 2015.
9   GreenWave, New Haven, Connecticut, 2025. A regenerative ocean farm that grows seaweed and shellfish. https://www.greenwave.org.
10 Nemo's Garden, Noli, Italy, 2025. Special underwater pods grow vegetables and fruits. https://nemosgarden.com.
11 Floating Dairy Farm, Rotterdam, Netherlands, 2025. A three-story dairy farm with milking cows. https://www.holland.com.
12 KeAi, 2024. China is the birthplace of fish farming. China is currently the largest producer of edible seaweed. https://www.keaipublishing.com/.
13 Dal Lake in Kashmir, India, 2025. Farmers grow a variety of vegetables on special bamboo rafts. https://wldb.ilec.or.jp/Display/html/3555.
14 San Fernando, Philippines, 2017. Floating farms are an alternative for both flood-prone and drought-prone areas in the country. https://www.sunstar.com.ph/more-articles/floating-gardens-as-alternative-farming-systems-for-flood-prone-areas.

Chapter 7

1   UN Food and Agriculture Organization (FAO), *Global Agriculture Towards 2050*, 2025, https://www.fao.org/home/en.

2 UN Food and Agriculture Organization, *Human Nutrition: Key to Health and Development*, 2025. https://www.fao.org/nutrition/en/.

3 USDA Economic Research, "Food Security in the U.S.—Key Statistics & Graphics," January 8, 2025.

4 Kotchakorn Voraakhom, "Grow Your Own: Urban Farming Flourishes in Coronavirus Lockdowns," *National Catholic Reporter*, April 15, 2020.

5 American Society of Landscape Architects (ASLA), 2012, https://dirt.asla.org/2012/05/09/urban-agriculture-isnt-new.

6 Robert Costanza, Professor of Public Policy at the Australian National University and cofounder of the International Society for Ecological Economics, 2025. https://www.isecoeco.org.

7 The Food Project, 2025. Offers a six-week youth program to grow and distribute food. https://thefoodproject.org.

8 Brooklyn Grange, Brooklyn, New York, 2025. Rooftop farm. https://www.brooklyngrangefarm.com.

9 Chicago Botanical Garden, 2025. Soil-based rooftop garden. Classes and Workshops. https://www.chicagobotanic.org/calendar.

10 Lester Brown, Growing Home, 2025. Organic farming. https://www.growinghomeinc.org.

11 City Farm, Chicago, 2025. Growing crops on urban vacant fields. https://theresourcecenterchicago.org/city-farm.

12 Acta Non Verba, Youth Urban Farm Project, 2025. Engages and strengthens young people's understanding of nutrition, food production, and healthy living, https://anvfarm.org.

13 Seattle, Washington, Rainier Beach & Wetlands Urban Farm, 2025. https://seattle.gov/parks/allparks/rainier-beach-urban-farm-and-wetlands.

14 2025. Foot Print Farms, Jackson, Mississippi, 2025, Dr. Cindy Ayers Elliott, founder. https://footprintfarmsms.com.

15 Urban American Farmer, 2025. Trisha Bates, founder. Farms School for Chefs. https://www.urbanamericanfarmer.com.

16 Planting Justice, East Oakland, California, 2025, https://plantingjustice.org/?srsltid=AfmBOoo4qFoUPsyo1FiEArlMfWJ6oUrjuSVXbV89Uaes9-aJ3OZzWCid.

17 The P-Patch, 2025. https://www.seattle.gov/neighborhoods/p-patch-gardening.

18 Common Good City Farm, Washington, DC, 2025. https://www.commongoodcityfarm.org.

Chapter 8

1 Cree Community Farm, Saskatchewan, western Canada, 2025, https://www.cbc.ca/news/canada/saskatchewan/food-forest-grand-opening-expansion-1.6147659.

2 Sole Street Farm, 2025. Sole Street farm transforms vacant urban land into street farms. solefoodfarms.com.

NOTES

3. Milpa Alta, 2025. Urban rooftop farming, https://en.wikivoyage.org/wiki/.
4. Columbia, 2025. Small family gardens. https://acimedellin.org/huertas-urbanas-y-rurales-son-en-medellin-una-alternativa-para-aumentar-la-seguridad-alimentaria/.
5. Cities Without Hunger, São Paulo, Brazil, 2025. Community gardens, school gardens, and greenhouses on public and private unused land. https://use.metropolis.org/case-studies/brasil-sao-paulo-community-gardens.
6. The Bolívar 1 Organoponic Garden, 2024, https://venezuelanalysis.com/interviews/urban-agriculture-in-the-center-of-caracas-a-conversation-with-glenda-vivas/.
7. Agripolis Farms, Paris, France, 2025. The largest urban farm in the world. HTTPs://agripolis.eu.
8. The Mudchute Park and Farm in East London, 2025. Farm raises animals and grows vegetables. https://www.mudchute.org.
9. The Edible City, Andemach, Germany, 2025. Growing vegetables is accessible for everyone. https://urbangreenbluegrids.com/projects/the-bible-city-andernach/.
10. Small plot gardens in Barcelona, 2025. In the city there are fifteen municipal gardens distributed in the ten districts. https://barcelonasecreta.com/en/urban-orchard-lottery/.
11. Community Garden of Via Gandusio, 2025. Via Gandusio is a housing complex north of Bologna, Italy. A community rooftop garden for a mixed community. https://una.city/nbs/bologna/community-garden-gandusio.
12. South Korea, Metro Farm, 2025. A hydroponic farm. https://www.downtowneast.com.sg/experience/shops/details/metro-farm.
13. Pakistan, Vertical Farming, 2025, https://una.city/nbs/karachi/pakistans-first-vertical-farm.
14. Urban Farming Practices in South Jakarta, Indonesia, 2023. https://una.city/nbs/jakarta/urban-farming-practices-south-jakarta.
15. India, 2025. https://www.edengreen.com/blog-collection/urban-agriculture-countries.
16. The Edible Garden City, Singapore, 2025. The mission: to inspire, engage, and make it possible for people to grow their own food in Singapore. https://www.ediblegardencity.com.
17. Future Fresh in Manila, Philippines, 2025. Aeroponic farm grows greens all year long. https://futurefresh.ph/collections/all.
18. Roger Royse, "Indoor Farming Companies Set Sights on China," *China Daily*, September 9, 2019.
19. Shanghai, China, 2004. Chinese organic farming pioneer Tony Zhang created the organic farm. https://matteroftrust.org/shanghai-organic-farm-made-from-78-recycled-shipping-containers/.
20. The Pasona Headquarters, Tokyo, Japan, 2005. A nine-story rooftop garden office building where employees can grow and harvest their own food at work. https://konodesigns.com/urban-farm/.
21. Farm Africa, Ethiopia, 2025, https://www.farmafrica.org/our-work/countries-we-work-in/ethiopia/.

Chapter 9

1. Cindy Hall, Iowa Agriculture Literacy Foundation, 2021. https://www.extension.iastate.edu/news/hall-hired-regional-director-iowa-state-university-extension-and-outreach.
2. World Wildlife Fund, 2025. The world's leading conservation organization. https://www.worldwildlife.org/about.
3. USDA Economic Research Service, "What Is Agriculture's Share of the Overall U.S. Economy?," December 19, 2024.
4. Future Farmers of America (FFA), 2023. The official name is the National FFA Organization. https://www.ffa.org/about/.
5. National Agriculture in the Classroom Organization, 2025. A free database of relevant, standards-based lesson plans that use agriculture as a context for science, social studies, and nutrition education content for K-12 classrooms. https://agclassroom.org.
6. American Farm Bureau Foundation for Agriculture, 2025. Our agricultural literacy resources and opportunities help bridge the gap between farmers, ranchers and the general public. https://www.agfoundation.org.
7. The National Agricultural Literacy Outcomes (NALOs), 2025. Benchmarks related to agricultural literacy. https://cdn.agclassroom.org/nat/data/get/NALObooklet.pdf.
8. U.S. Department of Agriculture (USDA), *Victory Gardens*, 2025. https://www.nal.usda.gov/exhibits/ipd/small/exhibits/show/victory-gardens/victory-garden-aids.
9. National Farm to School Network, 2025, https://www.farmtoschool.org.
10. Slow Food USA, 2025. https://slowfoodusa.org.
11. Green America Organization, 2025. Promotes environmental awareness. https://www.greenameria.org.
12. Debra Spielmaker, *Utah State TODAY*, December 25, 2012.
13. The Edible Schoolyard, 2025. Celebrating 30 years of edible education. https://edibleschoolyard.org.
14. Green Bronx Machine, 2023–2024. Brought programming to more than 120 new schools. https://greenbronxmachine.org.
15. Youth Farm Stand (YFS), 2025. Slow Food Denver and its partner, Denver Urban Gardens (DUG), developed a farm stand model on school grounds. https://slowfoodusa.org/youth-farm-stands/.
16. Big Green Learning Gardens, 2025. Big Green has helped people grow their own food with school and home-based programs. https://biggreen.org.
17. Standing Rock Sioux tribes of North and South Dakota, *Standing Rock Sioux Reservation*, 2025. https://www.standingrock.org.
18. Tuba City Primary School, 2025. K-5 school. https://tcusd.org/tces/.
19. Growing Minds, 2025. Farm to school connects children to local food and farms. https://growing-minds.org/about-growing-minds-and-farm-to-school/.

NOTES

20 Micro Family Farms, 2025. Urban farming. https://www.microfamilyfarms.com.
21 Francis Scott Key School, 2025, https://key.philasd.org.
22 Ministry of Human Resource Development (India), 2025. https://www.devex.com/organizations/ministry-of-human-resource-development-india-52556.

SELECTED BIBLIOGRAPHY

The following books are excellent references in the fields of agriculture, climate change, food and nutrition, and the importance of agriculture technology.

Baszile, Natalie. *We Are Each Other's Harvest: Celebrating African American Farmers, Land, and Legacy*. New York: Amistad, an imprint of HarperCollins Publishers, 2021. Baszile provides a variety of materials including photographs, essays, poems, and first-person stories that cover the agricultural history of Black people and their connection to American land.

Bittle, Jake. *Great Displacement: Climate Change and the Next American Migration*. New York: Simon & Schuster 2023. The book reports that it is not only the land and sea animals who are migrated to new environments because of climate change. But millions of people will also be displaced over the next 50 years as global warming gets worse.

Bloomberg, Michael, and Carl Pope. *Climate of Hope: How Cities, Businesses, and Citizens Can Save the Planet*. New York: St. Martin's Press/Macmillan Publishers, 2017. The authors explore climate change solutions that will make the world healthier and more prosperous. *Climate of Hope*, Bloomberg and Pope offer an optimistic look at the challenge of climate change, the solutions they believe hold the greatest promise, and the practical steps that are necessary to achieve them.

Carpenter, Novella, and Willow Rosenthal. *The Essential Urban Farmer*. New York: Penguin Group Publishers, 2011.The two successful urban farmers share their experiences and offer guidance and provide blueprints and details in how to design an urban farm.

Despommier, Dickson PhD. *The Vertical Farm. Feeding the World in the 21st Century*. New York: Picador Publishers, 10th Anniversary Edition, 2011.

Federico, Giovanni. *Feeding the World: An Economic History of Agriculture, 1800–2000*. (The Princeton Economic History of the Western World). Princeton, NJ: Princeton University Press, 2008.

Franklin-Wallis, Oliver. *Wasteland: The Secret World of Waste and the Urgent Search for a Cleaner Future*. New York: Hachette Books, 2023.

Gates, Bill. *How to Avoid a Climate Disaster: The Solutions We Have and the Breakthroughs We Need*. New York: Alfred A Knopf, 2021. Gates emphasizes to stop global warming and avoid the worst effects of climate; humans need to stop adding greenhouse gases to the atmosphere.

Henson, Robert. *The Thinking Person's Guide to Climate Change*. 2nd Edition. Boston: American Meteorological Society, 2019. Robert Henson is a meteorologist and writer at the Weather Company. He has been updating and covering global record highs and the Paris Agreement to cut greenhouse gases.

SELECTED BIBLIOGRAPHY

Hoffmann, Michael P., Carrie Koplinka-Loehr, and Danielle L. Eiseman. *Our Changing Menu*. Ithaca, New York: Cornell University Press, 2021.

Hyman, Mark. *Food Fix. How to Save Our Health, Our Economy, Our Communities, and Our Planet—One Bite at a Time*. New York: Little, Brown Spark, 2021. Mark Hyman, a leading physician, shows how our food economy could be reshaped to make us healthier.

Ladner, Peter. *The Urban Food Revolution, Changing the Way We Feed Cities*. Nanaimo, British Columbia, Canada: New Society Publishers, 2011.

Lomborg. Bjorn. *False Alarm: How Climate Change Panic Costs Us Trillions Hurts the Poor and Fails To Fix The Planet*. New York: Hachette Book Group, 2020.

Paarlberg Robert. *Resetting the Table. Straight Talk About the Food We Eat*. New York: Alfred A. Knopf, 2012. Consumers want to know more about their food—including the farm it came from, the chemicals used, the nutritional value, how the animals were treated, and costs to the environment.

Patel, Raj. *Stuffed and Starved: The Hidden Battle for the World Food System*. Brooklyn, New York: Melville House Publishing, 2008. Raj Patel, a fellow at Food First, provides an up-to-date report how the world has more than one billion people starving and more than a one billion who are overweight. He has traveled to four continents to investigate global food systems and the need to create a more democratic sustainable food system and to stop the exploitation of both farmers and consumers.

Penniman, Leah. *Farming While Black: Soul Fire Farm's Practical Guide to Liberation on the Land*. White River Junction, Vermont: Chelsea Green Publishing, 2018. The book includes chapters on urban farming, restoring degraded land with no-till tillage, compost soil ecology, cover crops and polycultures—grow more than one species at the same time. The book also provides how to plan your farm business.

Philpott, Tom. *Perilous Bounty: The Looming Collapse of American Farming and How We Can Prevent It*. New York: Bloomsbury Publishing, 2020.

Pogue, David. *How to Prepare for Climate Change: A Practical Guide to Surviving the Chaos*. New York: Simon & Schuster, 2020. Pogue suggests how to prepare for floods, fires, hurricanes, heat waves, and droughts. He notes that climate change is making farming are lot harder.

Robinson, Mary. *Climate Justice. Hope, Resilience, and the Fight for a Sustainable Future*. New York: Bloomsbury Publishing, 2018. Robinson presents stories of how a variety of people are taking an active role in facing the climate change crisis. Robinson was the former president of Ireland and a UN Special Envoy on Climate Change.

Spencer, Kati. *City Farming: A How to Guide to Growing and Raising Livestock in Urban Spaces*. Sheffield, England: 5m Publishing, 2017. Kati Spencer is a Master Gardener volunteer and a popular international gardening and homesteading speaker. Kari Spencer is an author, instructor, and an advocate for the art of urban farming. She is the owner of The Micro Farm Project, Phoenix, Arizona, USA.

White, Monica M. *Freedom Farmers*. Chapel Hill, North Carolina: The University of North Carolina Press, 2018. *Freedom Farmers* expands the historical narrative of the black freedom struggle to embrace the contributions of southern black farmers and the organizations they formed. Please note less than 2% of US farmers are Black.

Willis, Katherine. *Good Nature*. New York: Pegasus Books, 2024. The author provides scientific facts that nature watching of green spaces is an excellent habit with many benefits for us. Life with plants is a must.

Wu, Amy. *From Farms to Incubators: Women Innovators Revolutionizing How Our Food Is Grown*. Fresno, California: Craven Street Books, 2021. Amy Wu, award-winning journalist and the director of the documentary film *From Farms to Incubators*, reports how women entrepreneurs in agtech are developing technology that can improve food and farming systems.

INDEX

aeroponic farms, USA 82–3
    5 points Farm, Jacksonville, Florida 82
    LA Urban Farms, Los Angeles, California 82
    O'Hare Airport Garden, Chicago, Illinois 82
aeroponic farms, world 82–3
    France, Paris, Tower Farm 82
    Great Britain, Bristol, LettUs Grow 83
    Italy, Bergamo 83
    Singapore, Aero Green Technology Farm 83
aeroponics 80–3
    low pressure and high pressure systems 81
agriculture literacy 127–8
    in the classroom 129
agricultural literate 128–9, 140
agriculture technology, growing crops 52–7
    AeroVironment 52
    Daily Light Sensors 53
    drone technology 52
    Global Positioning System Technology (GPS) 57
    monitoring and data collection 53
    pest control 53
    Quantix 52
    robots 56–7
    soil moisture sensor 55
agriculture technology, harvesting seafood 60–2
    acoustics 61
    GPS fishing boats 61–2
    research ships 61–2
    saildrones 60
    satellite tags 61
    variable rate technology 52
agriculture technology, raising livestock 58–60
    3-D camera technology 60
    automatic feeding and water systems 60
    automatic weighing system for livestock 60
    electronic Identification of animals 59
    PastureMap, Grassroots Carbon 58–9
agriculture, worldwide industry 1–3
agrivoltaics 62
agroforestry 47
air quality, indoor and outdoor pollution 18–19
Altland, James 84
American Farm Bureau Foundation Agriculture (AFBFA) 128–9, 140
    Pillars of Agriculture Literacy 128–9
American Society of Landscape Architects (ASLA) 102
Andrews, Danielle 103–7
Antarctica, ice cores 7
aquaculture 64–5
    advantages and limitations 65
    seaweed farming 85–7, 91–4
aquaponic farms, USA 85–6
    California, Half Moon Bay, Quroboros Farms 86
    New Mexico, Santa Fe, FarmPod Shipping Container 85–6
    New York, Brooklyn, Edenworks 86
aquaponic farms, world 87–90
    Italy, Rome, The Circle Food & Energy Solution 87–90
    Japan, Fujisawa, Aquaponi Farm 91
    Puerto Rico, Fusion Farms 90–1

Singapore, Fairmount Singapore
and Swissotel 122
aquaponics, innovative technology 85–7
Australia 8, 27, 29
Australian Nuclear Science and
Technology Organization (ANSTO) 7
ice cores 7

Bangladesh, sea level rise 14
rooftop gardens 122
Big Green Learning Garden 135
Blue River Company, LettuceBot 56
Brazil, organic farms 116–17
Brooklyn Grange, urban farm 109
Brown, Les, Growing Home Farms,
Chicago, Illinois 110
buffer zones 46

California
urban farms 110–11
wildfires 15
California Department of Forestry and Fire
Protection (CALFIRE) 15
Canada, vertical farm 78
carbon dioxide emissions 23, 38, 59, 92
Equatic Company 59
carbon sequestration, storage of
carbon 40
carbon sink 35, 40
Cater, Melinda 49
Caucasus Glacier 10
Ceaser, David 53–6
China
seaweed farming 94–5
urban farms, vertical farms 123
climate 6–8
climate change 3–8
droughts 9–10
floods 11–12
sea level rise 14
wildfires 15–16
climate change impacts community
health 18
climate change impacts food security
17–18, 101
climate change impacts global food
production 101
crops 8–9

fisheries 13–14
livestock 12
climate change managing
agriculture technology (Agitech) 51–65
animal waste management 23
land management 51
reducing methane emissions 22–3
regenerative agriculture 37–49
sustainable management of forests 36
climatologists 7
Colorado River Basin 9, 32
Columbia
urban farms 116
composting 41
container farms, *see* shipping container
farms
Costanza, Robert 102
cover crops, rye, oats, winter wheat 41
carbon sequestration for crops soil
health 40
crop rotation 43
row covers 44
crops 9–16
corn 9
crop losses 9–16
rice 9, 48
wheat 9, 11
Crop Swap L.A. 39

daily light sensors 53
deforestation 34–35
drip irrigation 45
drone technology 52, 61, 108
droughts 9–10
crop losses 9
Africa, India, Mexico, Spain 10
Kansas, Nebraska, Texas 9

Edible City, Germany 118–19
Edible Garden City Singapore 122
Edible Schoolyard Project 133–4
Egypt, rooftop farms 124
Eisenhower, Dwight 38
Eldridge, Honor 17
Elliott, Cindy Ayers, Dr 112
Environmental Protection Agency (EPA) 2,
23, 141
Ethiopia, Farm Africa 125

INDEX

farmers' markets 48
farming, *see* agriculture
farm workers, outdoor workers 16
   health issues 23–4
   Lopez, Efraim 24–6
   wildfires, smoke exposure 16
Feeding America 17, 142
fertilizers 22, 27, 37–8, 52
fisheries 60–1
   acoustic sensing 61
   saildrones 60
   satellite tags 61
floating farms
   China 98
   India 99
   Mexico 100
   Netherlands, floating dairy farm 98
   Philippines 99
   Singapore 99
floods, USA 11
   Iowa 11
   Montana 11
   Minnesota 1
   Nebraska 11
floods, world 11–12
   Belgium 11
   Brazil 12
   China 11
   Germany 11
   Italy 12
   Japan 11–12
   Libya 11
   Netherlands 12
   Nigeria 12
   Pakistan 12
Food and Agriculture Organization (FAO) 5, 8, 17, 27, 79, 125
food deserts 48, 85, 103, 112
food insecurity 17–18
   health problems 18
Food Project 103
   Andrews, Danelle 103–4
   health and nutrition 103–4
food security 17
food waste 98, 131–133
Forest Declaration Assessment 35
forests 35–47
   agroforestry 47

carbon dioxide 35
carbon sequestration 40
carbon sink 35, 40
deforestation 34–5
deforestation affects wildlife
   environment 35
   REDD+ 36
   reducing emissions 36
   reforestation 47
Forever Green Initiative 144
Fortune Business Insights 68, 85
France, rooftop farms 82
freshwater resources 26–7
   groundwater 27
   surface waters 26–7

Gates, Bill 23
geothermal energy 62
Germany, urban farms 118–19
Ghana 125
glaciers 10
   Caucasus Glacier 10
global positioning system technology (GPS) 57–8, 61
   mapping, pests and weeds 58
global warming 21–3
Great Britain, aeroponic vertical farms 82–3
Green Bronx Machine 134
greenhouse aquaponics 85
greenhouse, Disney World Greenhouses 80
greenhouse geothermal energy 62
greenhouse (GHG) gas emissions 3, 7, 21–4, 35
greenhouse, Gotham Green Farms, New York 80
   nitrous oxides (N_2O) and methane (CH_4) 3
greenhouse, Wellspring Harvest Greenhouse, Massachusetts 80
Greenland 7
Green Our Planet 135
green walls 102
GreenWave Ocean Farm 96
groundwater 27–31
   Liza McDonough 29–31
   Ogallala Aquifer 27
   pollution 28

Growing Minds 136
Guardian Report, The 28

Hanging Gardens of Babylon 69
Hargins, Jamiah 39
health issues and nutrition 18–19
　indoor and outdoor pollution 19
　obesity 18
　severe heat stress 18
herbicides 41, 43, 48, 52
Hong Kong, rooftop farms 110
hydroponic farming 67–70
hydroponic farms 68–78
hydroponic greenhouses
　Gotham Greens, Brooklyn 80
　Wellspring Harvest Greenhouse of Springfield, Massachusetts 80
hydroponics 67–80
hydroponic vertical farms, USA 69–79
　Vertical Harvest Farms, Jackson Hole, Wyoming 69–76
hydroponic vertical farms, world 76
　Bahamas, Nassau 79
　Japan, Kyoto, Keihanna Techno Farm 77
　Singapore, Sky Greens' Vertical Farm 77
　United Arab Emirates (UAE), Bustanica 76

ice cores 7–8
　Andrew Smith, ANSTO 7–8
indigenous agriculture 43
　Opaskwayak Cree First Nation Farm, kiscikânis 78, 115
　The Three Sisters 43
insecticides 43
integrated pest management (IPM) 43
intercropping 42
India, vertical farms 120–21
Intergovernmental Panel on Climate Change (IPCC) 6
Intergovernmental Science-Policy Platform on Biodiversity and Ecosystem Services (IPBES) 34
Iowa, floods 11
Italy vertical farms 83

Japan, rooftop urban farm 123–4

Kenya, sack gardens 44
Kerry, John, Special Presidential Envoy for Climate 3, 21, 139

Lake Meade Reservoir 9
Lake Powell, Reservoir 9
land degradation 34
Libya, floods 11
Ling, Kai-Shu 83
Loggins, Mike 136
Lopez, Efraim 24–6

manure, compost 41
manure lagoons 23
manure management 44–5
McDonough, Liza 29–31
methane from animals 44–5
methane from manure 23
methane from rice 48
methane, NASA airborne technology tracking tools 58
Mexico, floating farms and rooftop gardens 100, 116
Micro Family Farms, Loggins, Mike 136
Minnesota, Forever Green Initiative 144
Mississippi, urban farms 112
Montana, floods 11
mulching, preserves soil from erosion 41
multiple cropping, maintaining and improving soil fertility 42

nanotechnology 63–5
National Aeronautics and Space Administration (NASA) 13–14, 58, 81–2
　Airborne Visible Infrared Imaging Spectrometer (AVIRIS) 58
National Agriculture in the Classroom, Spielmaker, Debra 133
National Agriculture Literacy Outcomes (NALO) 129
National Drought Mitigation Center 9
National Farm to School Network 131
National Geographic 34
National Institute of Food and Agriculture 2
National Oceanic and Atmospheric Administration (NOAA) 6, 13, 143
　NOAA Alaska Fisheries Science Center 60

INDEX

National School Garden Program (NSGP), Slow Food, USA 131
National Science Foundation (NSF) 7
National Water Quality Assessment (NAWQA) 27
Nebraska 9, 11, 27
Nevada, Green Our Planet 134
New York Farms 80, 86
    rooftop urban farm 109
Nigeria 12, 17, 28
nitrogen 22
    fertilizers 22
    nitrate pollution 22
    nitrous oxides 22
North America Drought Monitor (NADM) 10
No-till farming, more fertility and less erosion 40, 108, 132

ocean farming, seaweeds and shellfish 95
    Bangs Island Mussels 98
    GreenWave Ocean Farm 96
    Nemo's Garden 96–7
oceans 7, 13, 27
    acidification 13
Ogallala Aquifer 27
organic farms, USA
    Alemany Organic Farm, California 110
    Brooklyn Grange 109
    City Farm Organic Farm, Chicago 110
    Common Good City Farm, Washington 113–14
    Growing Home Organic Farmer, Chicago 110
organic farms, world
    Caracas 117
    Sao Paulo 116–17
Osinga, Ronald 92

Patz, Jonathan 3
Pesticides 24, 27–8, 37
Petrenko, Vasil 7
Pew Research Center 6
Philippines, seaweed farms 95
plant growth nutrients 22, 68
polytunnels, London 118
population growth 5, 37, 101
    food security and crisis 17–18
Puerto Rico, hurricanes 90–1

radiocarbon 7
rain gardens 46–7
REED+ 36
regenerative agriculture 37–43
    buffer zones 46
    composting 41
    mulching 41
    no–till farming 40
regenerative ocean farming 95–6
Ren, Charlene 33–34
    MyH2O Testing Network 33–4
renewable energy on the farm
    geothermal 62
    solar 62
    wind 62
rice, major world rice producers 48
rice, methane emissions 48
rice, sustainable production 48
rice, System of Rice Intensification (SRI) 48
Ritz, Stephen, Green Bronx Machine 134
robot technology 56–7
    fruit harvesting robots 57
    LettuceBot 56
    spraying and weeding 56
rooftop farming, USA 109–123
    Chicago, Windy City Harvest Program 109
    New York, Brooklyn Grange 109
rooftop farming, world 82–124
    Bangladesh, Dhaka 122
    Egypt, Cairo 124
    France, Tower Farm 82
    Hong Kong, Bank of America 110
    India, Bengaluru, Bihar, Delhi 120–1
    Italy, Bologna, community gardens 119
    Japan, Tokyo, Persona Urban Rooftop Farm 123–4
    Mexico, Mexico City, Milpa community farm 116
row covers 44

sack gardens, Kenya 44
sand dams 45–6
school gardens, India 137–8
    Ministry of Human Resources Development 137–8
school gardens, USA 129–37

by state 133–7
diet and nutrition 130
history 129
mitigate climate change 131
monitor school waste 132
sea level rise 14, 79, 101, 139
sea level rise, fisheries and crop losses 14
seaweed farming 91–5
  China 94–5
  Japan 95
  Philippines 95
  South Korea 95
  USA 94
  Zanzibar 95
seaweeds and products 93–4
Slow Food, USA 131
shipping container farms 78–9, 85–6
  advantages and limitations 79
  Eden farms, Bahamas 79
  FarmPod, USA 85–6
  NXTLVL farms, Philippines 79
Singapore, Sky Greens Vertical Farms 77
Smith, Andrew 7–8
Smithsonian magazine, water shortages 32
soil, carbon sequestration 40
soil erosion 42–3, 132
soil health 37, 47
Soil Health Institute 34
Soil-less technology 109
soil moisture sensors 55
soil, no-till 40
solar energy 62
soybeans 11
Spielmaker, Debra 133
surface water 26, 46
  pollution 27–8

Texas, wildfires 15
Three Sisters, indigenous farmers 43
The Circle Food & Energy Solutions, Italy 87–90
tower gardens and farms, USA
  California, LA Urban Farms 82
  Chicago, O'Hare Airport Garden 82
  Florida, Jacksonville, 5 Points Farm 82
tower gardens and farms, world

Bergamo, Italy 83
Paris, Tower Farm 350 82
Singapore, Fairmont Singapore and Swissotel 122

United Arab Emirates, vertical farming 76
United Nations 4, 8, 79, 107
United Nations Development Programme 10
United Nations Food and Agriculture Organization (FAO), see FAO
United Nations World Water Development Report 32
United States Department of Agriculture (USDA) 52, 68, 114
  Natural Resources Conservation Service 40
United States Economic Research Service (ERS) 101
United States Environmental Protection Agency (EPA) 2, 28
urban farming 102–25
  advantages 102–3
  agriculture technology 108–9
  regenerative growing practices 108
urban farms, future, community gardens, parking lots, balconies, rooftops, parking lots, greenwalls, greenhouses, and schoolyards 107
urban farms, USA 110–13
  California, Oakland, Acta Non Verba Youth Urban Farm Project 111
  California, Oakland, Planting Justice Urban Farm 113
  California, San Francisco, Alemany Farms 110
  Georgia, Atlanta, Metro Atlanta Urban Farm 111
  Illinois, Chicago, City Farm 110
  Illinois, Chicago, Growing Home Organic Farm 110
  Illinois, Chicago, Windy City Harvest Program, Chicago Botanic Garden 109
  Maryland, Baltimore, Real Food Farm 112
  Mississippi, Jackson, Foot Print Farms 112

INDEX

New York, Brooklyn Grange 109
Ohio, Cleveland, City Farm 111
Texas, Austin, Urban America Farmer 112–13
Washington, D.C., Common Good City Farm 113–14
Washington, Seattle, Ranier Beach and Wetlands Urban Farm 112
Washington, Seattle, P-Patch Community Garden Program 113
urban farms, world 116–25
  Bangladesh, Dhaha 122
  Brazil, Sao Paulo 116
  Canada, Saskatchewan, kiscikânis, Cree Community Garden 115
  Canada, Vancouver, Sole Food Street Farm 115–16
  China, Beijing 123
  China, Shanghai 123
  Colombia, Mendellin 116
  Egypt, Cairo, Schaduf farms 124
  Ethiopia 125
  France, Paris, Agripolis Farms 117
  Germany, Andernach, The Edible City 118–119
  Germany, Berlin, urban gardens 118
  Ghana 125
  Great Britain, London, Mudchute Park and Farm 118
  Great Britain, London, Spitalfields City Farm 118
  India, Bengaluru 120–1
  India Bihar 120
  India, Delhi 121
  India, Mumbai 121
  Indonesia 94, 120
  Italy, Bologna, Community Gardens Via Gandusio 119
  Kenya 125
  Mexico, Mexico City 116
  Mexico, Milpa Alta Borough 116
  Pakistan 120
  Philippines 95, 99, 122
  Singapore 83, 121–122
  Spain, Barcelona, small plot urban gardens 119
  Sub-Sahara, Africa, urban farms 124–5
  Venezuela, Caracas 117

Van Wingerden, Peter 98
vertical agriculture 67–78
  aeroponics technology 67
  hydroponics technology 68
  vertical growing crops in limited space 67
vertical farms 80–1
  advantages and limitations 83–4
vertical farms, USA
  Ohio, 80 Acres Farm 111
  Wyoming, Jackson Hole, Vertical Harvest Farms 69–76
vertical farms, world
  Canada, Opaskwayak Cree First Nation Vertical Farm 78
  Chengdu, Sichuan Province 78
  China 123
  Great Britain, LettUs Grow Farms 82–3
  India, Bengaluru 120–1
  India, Mumbai 121
  Italy, Bergamo 83
  Karachi 120
  Kyoto, Keihanna 77
  South Korea, smart vertical farms 119–20
  United Arab Emirates, Bustanica 76
Victory Climate Garden 132
Victory Gardens, WWII 129
Vilsack, Tom 37
Voraakhom, Kotchakorn 102

Washington Post 1
Washington, Seattle urban farms 112
Waters, Alice 133
weather 5–6, 9, 13
weeds 41, 43
wetlands 23, 47
  wetlands restoration 47
wheat 9, 11, 21
wildfires
  farm workers, outdoor workers 4, 16, 23–4
  smoke exposure 16
wildfires impact crop losses 15
wildfires, USA
  California, Dixie Fire 15
  Texas, Smokehouse Creek Fire 15–16

wildfires, world
   Australia 16
   Europe 16
wind breaks 46
wind energy 62
World Bank 21, 94, 145
World Business Council for Sustainable Development 17
World Resources Institute 32, 37

World Wildlife Fund 1, 3
Wyoming vertical farms 69–76

Yehia, Nona, Wyoming, Jackson Hole, Vertical Harvest Farms 69–76

Zambia, droughts 10
Zanzibar, Africa, seaweed farms 95

ABOUT THE AUTHOR

John F. Mongillo is a member of the National Science Teachers Association. He has a bachelor of science degree in general education, a bachelor of science degree in special education, and a master of science degree in science education.

John taught for several years in grades 4–9. In 2016–2017, John was the STEM/STEAM Coordinator at Christ the King Catholic School, Jacksonville, Florida. His publishing background includes editorial positions at Houghton Mifflin Company and McGraw Hill, including writing for young readers who subscribed to *My Weekly Reader*, a children's newspaper.

He is the author of *A Student Guide to Energy*, a five-volume reference series; *Teen Guides to Environmental Science*, a five-volume reference series; and *Nanotechnology 101*. John is a coauthor of *Encyclopedia of Environmental Science* and *Environmental Activists*.